ART

Louisiana Museum of Modern Art

Hayward Gallery

Museo Nacional Centro de Arte Reina Sofía

Roy Lichtenstein

ALL ABOUT ART

ROY LICHTENSTEIN – ALL ABOUT ART

Edited by Michael Juul Holm, Poul Erik Tøjner and Martin Caiger-Smith

© 2003 Louisiana Museum of Modern Art and the contributors
The Work of Roy Lichtenstein is © Estate of Roy Lichtenstein, New York,
and reproduced by agreement with the Estate and CopyDan, Billedkunst, Denmark
Graphic design: Michael Jensen
Cover illustration: Roy Lichtenstein: Golf Ball (detail). 1962 – Cat. No. 10
P. 1: ART. 1962 – cat. No. 8. P. 144: Reflections: Art. 1988 – Cat. No. 48
Photos of the works of Roy Lichtenstein by Kevin Ryan, Robert McKeever, Bent Ryberg,
Erma Estwick, Frank Kleinbach, Zindman/Fremont and Gamma One Conversions
Translations from the Danish by James Manley
Printed at Rosendahls Bogtrykkeri, Esbjerg
Paper: Arctic The Extreme 170 gms
ISBN 87-90029-85-2
Printed in Denmark 2003

This catalogue is published on the occasion of the exhibition
Roy Lichtenstein – All About Art
Curated by Poul Erik Tøjner, Louisiana Museum of Modern Art

Louisiana Museum of Modern Art, Denmark
22 August 2003 – 11 January 2004
Exhibition Coordinator: Marianne Ahrensberg

Hayward Gallery, London
26 February – 16 May 2004
Hayward Gallery showing organized by Martin Caiger-Smith
assisted by Clare Hennessy

Museo Nacional Centro de Arte Reina Sofía, Madrid
24 June – 27 September 2004
Exhibition Coordinator: Verónica Castillo Díaz

 Main Sponsor of Louisiana's exhibitions 2001-2005

 Sponsor of the exhibition
at Museo Nacional Centro de Arte Reina Sofía

LENDERS

Fondation Beyeler, Riehen/Basel, Switzerland

The Brant Foundation, USA

The Eli and Edythe L. Broad Collection, USA

Collection Agnes Gund, New York, USA

Collection Charles Simonyi, Seattle, USA

Collection Gian Enzo Sperone, New York, USA

Collection Robert H. Halff, USA

Collection Steve Martin, USA

Joseph Helman, New York, USA

Kunsthaus Zürich, Switzerland

Kunstsammlung Nordrhein-Westfalen, Düsseldorf, Germany

David Lichtenstein, USA

Roy Lichtenstein Foundation Collection, New York, USA

Gordon Locksley and Dr. George T. Shea Collection, USA

The Museum of Contemporary Art, Los Angeles, USA

Museum Ludwig, Cologne, Germany

Louisiana Museum of Modern Art, Denmark

Museum für Moderne Kunst, Frankfurt am Main, Germany

National Gallery of Art, Washington, USA

Robert and Jane Rosenblum, New York, USA

San Francisco Museum of Modern Art, USA

Sonnabend Gallery, New York, USA

Tate, London, UK

Ulmer Museum, Ulm, Germany

Walker Art Center, Minneapolis, USA

Whitney Museum of American Art, New York, USA

Yale University Art Gallery, New Haven, CT, USA

And private collections

Contents

Foreword

When Roy Lichtenstein was asked why he painted pictures of pictures, his reply was that artists had, in a sense, always done so. In the past, when the artist sat in front of his model and painted her, his ambition was to transform her into a picture. But the most important thing was *the picture* – not the model. The good artist wants to make a good picture. And that is why a *model* is a perfectly reasonable starting-point.

Lichtenstein turned his gaze in two directions: to the great archive of pictures in the history of art, and to the riotously proliferating image bank of contemporary American culture. His claim about the images of art history was that many of them stand out so strongly that they have imprinted themselves in our minds as a kind of artistic logo, just as particular genres and subjects have: still lifes, landscapes, pictures from the artist's studio and so on. And his interest in images from popular culture had to do precisely with the power of the style – whether in the simple representation of a thing – a washing machine, a pair of sneakers, a hotdog – or in the more sentimentally artful melodramatic representation of feelings and conflicts in which the comic strip excelled.

In both cases Lichtenstein was looking for the same thing: a strong, clear image that people could immediately recognize. And that is what his pictures undeniably are: sharp, precise, strong in colour and surface. Here there is no painterly muddiness, no 'Nordic light' or Romantic twilight, no brushstrokes, no trace of the painter's doubting soul, trembling hand or ecstatic gesture. On the contrary, Lichtenstein's universe is coolly mechanical, his art based on graphic precision and compositional strength.

What Lichtenstein wanted to point out was how important it is for modern man to know the difference between pictures and reality: if we start to identify with all the pictures that are out there trying to convey ideas and impose models, patterns of consumption, concepts of beauty, criteria for success and objects of desire on us, then we lose our grip on reality. And that is in fact why Lichtenstein keeps on painting reality so that it looks artificial. For only that way do we learn to recognize a model when we see one.

The more Lichtenstein's pictures look like what they represent, the less they look like them in reality. Lichtenstein transforms our world into logos and trademarks for experiences while he – in reality – is an old-fashioned, moral artist who does so in order to warn us against letting reality merge with our images of it. That is of course why he keeps returning to the image as image.

The artist's lifelong fascination with and investigation of the image as image is the pivotal point in *Roy Lichtenstein – All About Art*. This is clearly reflected in the large group of pictures in which different elements in the rhetoric of image formation are exposed: his brushstrokes, stretchers, mirrors, paraphrases of other paintings, self-portraits and, finally, purely declamatory statements such as *ART* and *Image Duplicator*. All around this Lichtensteinian epicentre we find other important groups of works: the early pictures of objects and clichés, flat iconic representations of archetypal scenarios from popular culture, as well as consumer culture's transformation of things into images. And finally – in contrast to the emphatic surface – Lichtenstein's equally enduring interest in space and spatiality: landscape, still life, interiors as well as the mental space that unfolds with a clear nod to Surrealism.

Lichtenstein never abandoned his fundamental interest in the power of the image. It can be found everywhere in his work, as an essential feature of his style, which has quite naturally become one of the most unmistakable trademarks in the history of art.

Roy Lichtenstein's painting is, in other words, a reminder of the capabilities – and limitations – of the image; most beautifully realized in his use of what we call – with a word that comes from the printing trade – a cliché: the image that is so strong that it can be used again and again, but which on the other hand is empty; a combination that is both important and highly instructive.

It may well be that Donald Duck's beak is shorter today than in 1961, when Lichtenstein depicted him on his fishing trip with Mickey, but the artist's concern with the relationship between viewer and image which the picture manifests has not lost currency. On the contrary: Lichtenstein's cheerful and yet subtle analysis of our cultural icons seems at least as relevant today – when even the telephone has capitulated to the image – as it did in the sixties.

The cooperation of the Roy Lichtenstein Foundation has been crucial to the genesis of this exhibition. Since the very first visit to Washington Street in New York, we have benefited from the interest, commitment, generosity, unique professionalism and invaluable advice of Executive Director Jack Cowart and Managing Director Cassandra Lozano, the Registrar Natasha Sigmund and Shelley Lee, Intellectual Property Rights Manager for the Estate. Our warmest thanks too to Dorothy Lichtenstein for her involvement and active support, as well as to Mitchell Lichtenstein and David Lichtenstein. We must add out heartfelt thanks to the many lenders to the exhibition – private as well as institutional – who have all made invaluable contributions to *Roy Lichtenstein – All about Art*.

It has been equally crucial for Louisiana to be able to work from the start with two partners who demonstrated an interest in Lichtenstein at the same time as Louisiana – the Hayward Gallery in London and the Reina Sofía museum in Madrid. It has thus once more been a great pleasure for Louisiana to have established the international cooperation that is so important to Danish culture, and which Louisiana sees as its special mission to maintain and develop. Thanks to the Director Juan Manuel Bonnet and to the then Deputy Director Enrique Juncosa for their early declared interest in the exhibition, and to Susan Ferleger Brades, Director of the Hayward Gallery, for her commitment. Our special thanks must go too to Martin Caiger-Smith, Head of Exhibitions at the Hayward Gallery, for his close involvement with both the exhibition and the catalogue. Thanks, finally, to my assistant on the exhibition, Marianne Ahrensberg, for her untiring, accurate and never-failing work; to Museum Curator Anders Kold, Louisiana, who was involved with the first phase of the organization of the exhibition; and to Head of Publications Michael Juul Holm for his work with the catalogue, and to its graphic designer Michael Jensen. And thanks too to the contributors to the catalogue – to Michael Lobel, Jack Cowart and Avis Berman. Finally we are very pleased to be able to include in the catalogue David Sylvester's last interview with Roy Lichtenstein. And in conclusion, my thanks to Louisiana's principal sponsor 2001-2005, DONG.

Poul Erik Tøjner
Director
Louisiana Museum of Modern Art

Preface

Roy Lichtenstein first exploded into the consciousness of the British public when his majestic and monumental painting *Whaam!*, of 1963, was bought by the Tate Gallery in 1966. Two years later, when the Tate mounted a Lichtenstein retrospective, the first solo exhibition ever presented there of a living American painter, its then Director, Norman Reid, remarked that the purchase had 'aroused more public interest than almost any purchase since the war'. That this debate was framed around questions such as – was this art? were comic strips an admissible source of imagery for serious painters? – demonstrates the relative innocence of the British gallery-going public at the time, and the extraordinary power of Lichtenstein's work to command attention, through the sheer force of its content, the clarity of its composition, the boldness of its colour and its scale. For a generation of gallery-goers in the 1960s, *Whaam!* stood as the ultimate image of the New in art.

London's acquaintance with Lichtenstein's work soon grew; he was included in the Hayward's exhibition of Pop Art in 1969, and a number of commercial gallery exhibitions followed in the 1980s and 1990s, as Lichtenstein entered the mainstream of international contemporary art.

Meanwhile, major public exhibitions were mounted here of a number of Lichtenstein's contemporaries: notably at the Hayward Gallery itself, with Jasper Johns in 1978 and 1990, Claes Oldenburg in 1996 and, in 1989, Andy Warhol, the 'twin pillar' of Pop Art, along with Lichtenstein, whose career was again celebrated in London in 2002. These exhibitions presented a deeper, developed picture of those artists' trajectories over thirty or more years, but Lichtenstein, despite his unassailable international reputation, has until now not been seen here in comparable fashion.

The Hayward has wanted very much to rectify this. Our exploration of the possibilities of mounting an exhibition brought us into contact with colleagues at the Louisiana Museum of Modern Art and the Museo Nacional Centro de Arte Reina Sofía, who were harbouring similar ambitions and, happily, similar ideas on the scope and direction of a project. We all also elicited firm support and enthusiasm from the Roy Lichtenstein Foundation. The resulting collaboration on this exhibition, which has been developed and led by the Louisiana Museum, has been a rewarding experience, and confirmed our conviction that this is the right moment to look afresh at Lichtenstein's art.

8

The exhibition focuses on Lichtenstein's imagery, as it developed from the 1960s to his death in 1997, in paintings and works on paper, and seeks to counter the relatively time-bound view of Lichtenstein as just a Pop artist. It fuses genres and series through which Lichtenstein worked over years, positioning the Pop works of the early 1960s with the work of following decades, and revealing them as a continuum. In so doing, it locates Lichtenstein's originality less in the novelty of Pop Art than in the sustained and complex interrogation of the nature of the painted image in the modern world which he pursued with integrity and inventiveness over thirty years. Lichtenstein emerges, through this, as a classical artist, whose faith in the potential of painting to convey something specific and important survived even his own penetrating analysis of its limits, as well as its possibilities. Such an achievement has, surely, much to tell a new generation of artists, as well as a new public encountering the range of Lichtenstein's paintings for the first time.

We are deeply grateful to our colleagues at the Louisiana Museum of Modern Art, and in particular to its Director Poul Erik Tøjner, for creating an exhibition which combines a depth and authority with a radical and original perspective on Lichtenstein entirely appropriate to the artist's intentions and rigour. We join them in our gratitude to the artist's widow, Dorothy Lichtenstein, and to Jack Cowart and his colleagues at the Roy Lichtenstein Foundation, whose advice and support have been essential, and generously given, throughout; and to the exhibition's many lenders, whose willingness to support the exhibition at each of its three showings is deeply appreciated.

As ever, I am grateful to all my colleagues who have helped bring this exhibition to fruition at the Hayward. I pay particular tribute to Martin Caiger-Smith, the Hayward's Head of Exhibitions, who has immersed himself in Lichtenstein, contributed to the exhibition's curatorial perspective and to this book and overseen the London showing of the exhibition, ably supported by his assistant Clare Hennessy.

Susan Ferleger Brades
Director
Hayward Gallery

62.
Knock Knock. 1961
Sonnabend Collection

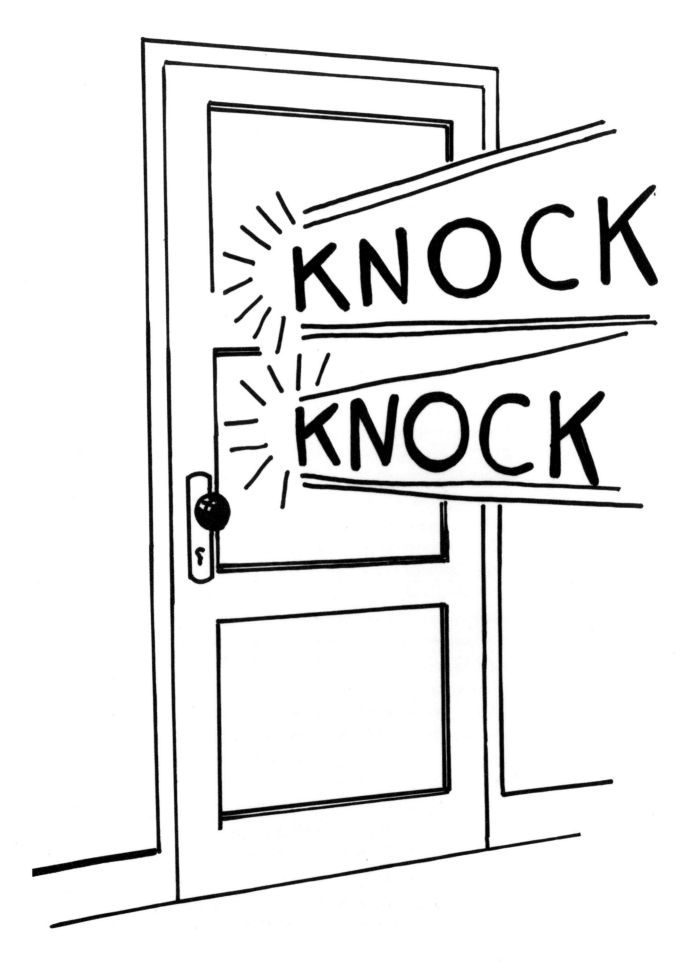

Poul Erik Tøjner

I know how you must feel...

Knock, knock.
"...some visiter... tapping at my chamber door –
Only this and nothing more..."[1]
Well, it's unlikely to be a raven standing on the other side of the door in Roy Lichtenstein's drawing from 1961. So who is it?

If the drawing were (re)instated in the narrative sequence in which it is a *locus classicus,* we could imagine well enough how the surrounding scenes would look. The following frame would show the reaction on our side of the door: a face expressing surprise, anticipation, fear – in short, a response. The next would have the door opening, and depending on the genre's affinity with the thriller, a revelation would come after extended creaking, suspense and delay. The last scene would be an encounter, and the response would now be a matter of reality, no longer of expectancy: the end of the world, the beginning of my life – secret police – *mon amour* – room service.

But Lichtenstein is no narrator. The figurative surface is a deceit. I am the narrator. Lichtenstein himself is a narratologist – with the picture as an analytical device. His narratives are about narratives and the potential of pictorial narration. In other words, the small drawing is an allegory, an allegory of the horizon of the visual message – at once testamentary and prophetic. Something precedes the picture – and something follows after. The picture itself is only an intersection that dramatizes the viewer's relationship with it.

The history of art is full of such doors – and, for that matter, windows. They pretend to lead either into the truth of the picture or back to the source from which the scene arises, or else they disclose new worlds that burst open the limited space of the image. As with Magritte – whose latest update can be seen in the film *The Matrix Reloaded,* in which the protagonist, Neo, opens the door in the metropolitan palace of the Merovingian only to find the Alps on the other side. The door is an iconic augmentation, which almost always refers back to the picture's own intent as a picture: to widen the horizon of the spectator.

And yet Lichtenstein is no Magritte either. His door is not one of the traditional doors of perception, for the sober black-and-white drawing has to be read, not felt. The sound is on our side of the door: "Knock, knock". But it comes from somewhere else.

What you see is not what you hear. You see a trace, a sign – but its origin is blocked off. In other words you see something that isn't there. What you see is what you don't see.

Knock, knock is an allegory of the picture's pact with the invisible. And it points to the heart of Lichtenstein's art, which revolves around the paradox of visibility: the clearer the figures appear in his work, the more they are hidden. Not hidden in any metaphysical sense as with the Expressionists, where there is also paradox inherent in the physical quality of the painting whereby the painter creates light and space by covering the canvas more and more: in Lichtenstein's work it is the dazzling clarity and precision of its hyperreality that permits the picture to conceal the world from us by being a model of it. The more it looks like it, the less it looks like it.

So is it Roy who's knocking? No, not at all. Roy is on our side of the door – he is always on the viewer's side. That's the only position for Lichtenstein; which is why his self-portrait can be found in the explosion – a concentration of absence, a representation of what has just been here (holy smoke!) – or in the mirror, in which anyone can be reflected, including the artist.

Two focal points in the ellipse of the self are scattered generously through Lichtenstein's work. First, presence as pure, explosive energy, at the expense of the loss of the figure: Lichtenstein returns persistently to this theme, expressed for the first time in *Popeye*, 1961, and most recently in a late sketch for a *Last Supper* for the Padre Pio Pilgrimage Church, designed by Renzo Piano, where the 'presence' of Christ is depicted as an explosive crystal of light. Secondly, the mirror – a Lichtenstein leitmotif *par excellence,* whether we are talking about real, tangible mirrors or the general use of a mirroring mechanism that permits anyone to be repeated in 'the image duplicator': the other artists – Picasso, Léger, Mondrian – but also Lichtenstein himself, redone by Lichtenstein.

II

That Roy Lichtenstein's work is about art and about the artist is something anyone can see. This isn't the subtle allusion of modernist self-reflection: Lichtenstein gets right up front in his thematization of art-as-art. It's all about art. The thematization comprises the myth of the artist at all levels – from the talk-of-the-town sociological chic of *Masterpiece*, 1962, through the many unmasked references to the artistic illusionist's craft

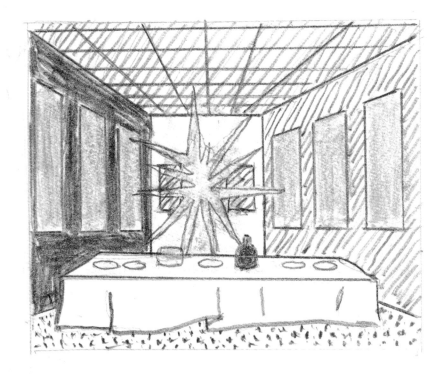

85.
Study for Chapel
of the Eucharist, Padre Pio
Pilgrimage Church. 1997
Private Collection

(stretchers, brushstrokes, entablatures) to quotations and self-quotations, paraphrases and even literal translations.

It is tempting to view Lichtenstein's activities in this field as harmonizing with the self-referential turn, the focus on aesthetic meta-language that several of Lichtenstein's contemporaries took from Marcel Duchamp; but it is unfortunately also easy to over-look a number of factors in this artistic self-fertilization. The easiest course would be to see art-about-art as a purely formalist stage of development in a narrative about the evolving autonomy of art and the corresponding loosening of its links with the world. Lichtenstein himself contributes to this by emphasizing the formal over content in his artistic endeavours.

It can hardly be a violation of personal integrity to look slightly beyond, or around, Lichtenstein's statements on his work and aims. As the intentions of Lichtenstein's work have become clearer in retrospect, the artist's own statements on it have become more open to question. For it is far from true that art-about-art reflects a definitive loss of subject and experience, and thus a fundamental bankruptcy in art's dealings with reality. Rather, art-about-art is about the *contemporary* possibility of speaking of certain things. And surely no one would deny that Lichtenstein's art is full of certain things – love and war, objects and spaces, conventions, traditions, genres – in short, standard fundamental phenomena. And it is the *relations* with these phenomena – and the ex-periences historically associated with these phenomena – that are channelled into reflections upon the possibilities of art.

Lichtenstein's choice of style (if style is something you choose) and of subject is very often associated with a kind of high/low issue. On the basis of a notion – antiquated in itself – of decorum in the vocabulary of cultural expression, Lichtenstein is repre-sented as an artist who reaches out and *down* for both theme and form. 'Commercial' is by definition 'low'; 'superficial' (surface-orientated) representation is base or shallow in contrast to the depths of the heights – and explanations of Lichtenstein's plunges into the surface range from the internal, art-historical – the showdown with Abstract Ex-pressionism – to the more external, cultural historical, where the burgeoning of mass culture and the increasing image explosion of the real world are cited as the inspira-tional basis for a new 'decorum'.

Of course there is some truth in all these explanations. The Greenbergian cul-de-sac had inspired young artists to venture out on to the open street, and of course the heroic pathos of Abstract Expressionism must have taken on the look of mere postu-late, at the point at which it appeared to be something that had to be *learned* by a new generation. Once something has been exposed as rhetoric, the *choice* of a *different* rhetoric is at least possible, and for those who came to realize that they were not one of the Abstract Expressionist elect, the choice of something *different* actually became a new imperative.

In hindsight, now that the idea of decorum no longer has any meaning in connec-tion with art, it is clear that Lichtenstein did not want to use his choices to explode the concept of art by extending it once again towards new indecorous horizons, but rather wanted to explore the possibility of using the picture as a mode of awareness. This was his main goal – to believe in the meaningfulness of painting pictures, and the ability of the visual image to say something that cannot be said in any other way. For the same reason his relationship with his subjects became more than peripheral – they were not simply pretexts for painting.

Painting is in fact about the possibility of saying certain things. This is the chal-lenge – rather than simply reducing art *ad absurdum* again in the eternal revolt against *je-ne-sais-quoi.* Without comparing the two in other ways, it was as true of Lichtenstein, as it was for Philip Guston when he succeeded in creating figurative painting for the second time in his life in 1971, that the challenge was to let painting play a role, not to be played out in its role.

13

III

When Lichtenstein's art 'arrived' in the early 1960s it caused a sensation, and in a riposte to the famous interview with Jackson Pollock which proposed him as America's greatest artist, Lichtenstein was proposed in a parallel article in *Life* magazine in 1964 as the nation's worst. The critical voices – then and later – fall into two groups: one concerned with the artist's attitude to what is represented, one with the specificity of representation itself.

With the former we have the classic politicizing reflections on whether Pop Art affirms or critically opposes the consumer society from which it draws its subjects and its style. Objections can be directed equally at Lichtenstein and Warhol, and they can take different twists and turns depending on one's dialectical talent or feeling for the paradoxes of negativity.[2] Warhol fuels the criticism with his consistent nihilistic largesse, while Lichtenstein's seemingly innocent or naive dealings with the imagery of capitalism appear to convict him of 'false consciousness' before all the tribunals. Today, when consumerism itself has developed a variety of critical stances – on the quality of the consumed, for example – few would see Lichtenstein's fascination with the product as anything more than a means to depict a new reality that has long since been overtaken by a cyberspace in which the object-as-fetish has been superseded by pure availability.

Those more concerned with the specificity of representation object to the apparent lack of transformation in Lichtenstein's work, its close relation to its source imagery or objects. Lichtenstein defended himself by saying that artists do not 'transform' what they see, they simply create their work as they see it – an excellent argument that can be supported by what we, the viewers, see if we look at the 'originals': that Roy Lichtenstein does in fact transform to a great extent – if that were really to be the crux of the matter.

All the source material that Lichtenstein uses crucially changes character under his sure hand and sure eye for compositional unity. And the evidence is clear, for Lichtenstein, with his closeness to the source images from which he drew and to the traditions he is mimicking – the tradition of art history as well as that of the comic strip – is precisely *not* trying to conceal his dependence on the model in any way. On the contrary, identifying it is vital[3], inasmuch as any comparison with the source material documents how the artist adds, subtracts, intensifies and, in a word, unifies his subject matter into – well, into a subject.

In other words you could choose to defend Lichtenstein in the courtroom with various observations and affidavits, or – probably easier – you can stick to rather banal jargon about the death of the notion of originality. In reality I prefer the former approach, because it insists that Lichtenstein works with a belief in the special energies and potential of the visual medium, while the latter argument – the deconstruction of the idea of originality – all too often leads to a laxness that is quite incompatible with the consistency and passion with which the allegedly unoriginal artist takes his point of view to the market. Then at least you avoid *that* pathetic antinomy.

There is no doubt – for me at least – that Lichtenstein, however we view his work, transports the image into a philosophical space after airing it in the banal, recognizable universe of hot-dogs and washing machines, and that – as will become evident – it is the banality and the dedicated object-ness that permit the picture to stand as an object of the viewer's reflection. The less that happens in a picture, the more we are forced to deliberate on the effect of its actual visuality.

IV

Lichtenstein was interested in pictoriality as such. He was fascinated by the nature of the picture as communication – that is, its relation to what was outside it, to the viewer, just as he was deeply involved in clarifying the picture's wellsprings from within, or from wherever it had its origin. And his work is consequently organized around a quite radical exploration of what pictoriality really is – both for an artist and for an ordinary person in the modern world. It is of course not so surprising – much less original – that a visual artist of all people should devote his reflections to this issue. Who else should? But

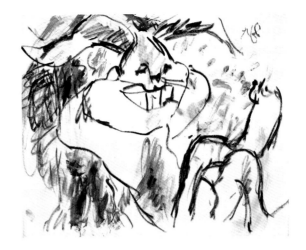

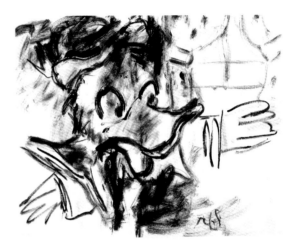

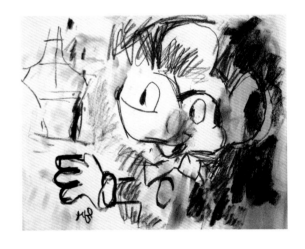

56.
Bugs Bunny. 1958
Private Collection

57.
Donald Duck. 1958
Private Collection

58.
Mickey Mouse I. 1958
Private Collection

14

Lichtenstein's work nevertheless focuses to a rare degree on the issue of sight or vision. There are very few pictures in his oeuvre that do not deal with it – in fact, there is no innocent image.

Pictoriality is two things for Lichtenstein: it is an open-ended history of art in which he is enmeshed as a professional visual artist; and it is a flow in which you can observe the state and progress of society.

As for the history of art, Lichtenstein confirms with his paraphrases of the works of other artists that this history lies likes a kind of cultural DNA within us. Images from past art are no longer pictures of some illusionistic reality outside the window of the artist; Lichtenstein's images *from* the history of art are images *of* the history of art.

Before we get too pleased with this notion of the apparent autonomy of art, we must remember that it is Lichtenstein who so to speak creates it, by pointing out how history is something produced by the individual or by the achievement of a collective culture; that is, by wresting from history idioms which will then crystallize into historical evidence, and which in the course of this crystallization or incarnation will assume the status of the historical *per se.*

The history of art thus becomes the history of history, and can then be celebrated as a kind of nature – a process to which Lichtenstein contributes quite uniquely in his paraphrases – from Monet through Mondrian to Picasso – both when he eliminates the original painter's signature (the concrete signature and texture-as-signature) and consequently elevates the mode of representation into a kind of typology – the Mondrianesque, the Picassoesque or the Monetesque – and thus also forces upon the viewer an uncomfortable awareness of a culture in which we, as culture-identifying individuals, perhaps see a work by Picasso more as 'a Picasso' than as the singular work it is. (On the other hand this can be a godsend to the museum director who wants the public to flock through the doors and confirm the museum's status as a mass medium.)

As for the second point – the development of visual media in Western capitalist society – Lichtenstein is equally perspicacious as observer, explorer and stage manager. With his incorporation of the iconography and methods of the printed media, with his fondness for the communicative image in an extended sense – where the word 'communication' means not only message but also figuration, recognizability, lucidity – Lichtenstein widens the resonating surface of artistic self-reflection to include the world in which the viewer really moves, the world that art has often set out to transform or transcend.

In so doing, he achieves two things: first, he shows that the commonplace actually *is* an ongoing transfiguration. Advertising, pornography and the media, for example, deploy methods that can in no way be called different in essence from those of art – although the ways in which they are used are not necessarily the same. And secondly, Lichtenstein as an artist is a courageous man since he meets these conventional antitheses of art at the point where they are most similar in order – at this very point – once more in the historical perspective, to let art *add* something. For just as no one – at least today – is in any doubt that Lichtenstein made a substantial contribution to the history of western European art with his pictures, no one should be in any doubt either that the marked resemblance of his oeuvre to existing pictures was brought about precisely to evoke the difference between them!

It is precisely the striking resemblance that creates the difference – and it is precisely the resemblance that deflates any petty criticism that Lichtenstein simply imitated or duplicated masterpieces of art alongside the icons of popular culture. It was by being as demonstrative and precise as he was that Lichtenstein showed that he was far beyond both the myth of originality and the critique of originality. His work as a whole is one great *demonstratio ad oculos* of a far-reaching concept of pictoriality and visuality. The question for Lichtenstein is thus not where painting stands within painting, but what kind of image painting is – and in a broader sense what kind of image the artistic image is.

V

What sounds like a metaphysical-aesthetic issue therefore became for Lichtenstein something far more concrete. In reality his interest in the picture as both an art-historical entity and a social impulse liberated him from the temptation of dogmatically associating art with 'new' projects or areas of specific evolutionary legitimacy. Pop Art was thus a method that the artist adopted; it was not in itself – at any rate not for Lichtenstein – a new school of artistic thought intended to supersede an old one. Lichtenstein saw himself, significantly, as a classical artist who worked with issues familiar as far back as the Renaissance, and this confirms that his fundamental interest in the creation of images was more important to him than asserting himself as a contemporary artist.

It is against this background that we should view his now well-known and undoubtedly formative period of study under Professor Hoyt Sherman, at the Ohio State University in the late 1940s, and especially the odd mixture of experimental ingenuity and positivistic enthusiasm – no big deal actually, simply scientific opportunity![4]

Hoyt Sherman's experiments pointed in two essentially contrary directions: his work at the "Visual Demonstration Center" showed how our visual sensory apparatus provides the viewer with various items of information about objects depending on their internal relations in space. This relativity of the sensory process was countered by another type of experimentation, the work of fine-tuning artistic compositional competency in the so-called Flash Lab.

Sherman's idea was to use kinaesthetic experiments to confirm the role of the hand as a direct extension of the mind. The experiments placed a number of people in the Flash Lab, where very brief exposures of objects in an otherwise dark room were to trigger off a mental after-image which was immediately to be drawn, still in the dark, by those present – and without visual 'corrections'. The drawing would thus document a simultaneity of hand and mind, which would in turn provide a value-framework for the artistic image – in terms of its ability to unify what otherwise seemed fragmented. The philosophy was harmonistic, although it was also mechanistic, and all in all it was meant to enhance the individual's general visual preparedness.

The world that was dissolved before the eyes in the 'Visual Demonstration Center' was put together again by the unifying capacity that the students refined during training in the Flash Lab. In certain contexts, the two experiences are two sides of the same thing – at least in the new and technologically intensified perceptual space that is taken to its peak in the military-industrial context. Hoyt Sherman's investigations were related to the increasing demands made on fighter pilots who had to identify enemy planes at high speeds and focus on them in a combat situation – a specific angle which of course assumed its place in Lichtenstein's many war pictures, where the monocular, concentrated gaze through the sights or periscope becomes an allegory of the easiest type of unification. Lichtenstein later reversed this focus in his penchant for interiors whose indeterminability is established by reflections, Benday shading and the perturbations of disconnected scale relationships.

VI

Roy Lichtenstein's time with Hoyt Sherman not only helped to enhance his feeling for the sister disciplines of visual art, gestalt and perception psychology; their pragmatic dimension certainly also honed Lichtenstein's sense of how much the visual idiom depends on various kinds of mechanical manipulation. And although his studies were aimed primarily at the development of a kind of controlled response to visual stimuli – a response that was to confirm the synthesizing power of the image – his experiences inevitably provided him with as much critical as educational data: for example a problematization of the notion that impression can be directly converted into expression, ideally viewed as a kind of automatic writing, but without the heterogeneous background of automatism where it is alien, or occult forces that control the expression, regardless of the conventions of the normal picture. And in this sense the studies – irrespective of their other theoretical consequences – became an intellectual component in Lichtenstein's art, whose function was to provide the image with effective performative power beyond an expressivist paradigm.

So a direct line runs from Sherman's perfectible perception to Lichtenstein's compositional feeling for clear visual communication – disregarding all the calculations in between. And as always – for the allegorist Lichtenstein – the knowledge gained was not only a means of developing the images further; it also invaded the pictures, which for a while had to be vehicles for themes explicitly drawn from Hoyt Sherman's monocular philosophy. Many of Lichtenstein's pictures, for example, comment on the stability and certainty of one-eyed perspective: from *I Can See the Whole Room... And There's Nobody In It!*, 1961, which seems like a veritable look into the Flash Lab itself – where there is exactly *nothing*, because the physical, corporal, human eye, with all its uncertainty, has been suspended in favour of the mechanically trained receptor – to the many war scenes, where efficiency is directly proportional to the degree of one-eyedness.

With Hoyt Sherman's disciplining of visual competence in one hand and institutionalized art history in the other, Lichtenstein could view the medium of painting from both sides and sum up its possibilities and status by asking two questions. How does one create pictures with a maximum of performative power (a question that arises from observing both the commercial culture industry and the established art industry)? And what kind of identificatory surface does the picture become? Intellectual artist as he always was, Lichtenstein answered these questions in several ways. He practised with examples, he worked through these questions, and he commented on his pictorial philosophy *with* pictures – i.e. in the form of allegories of the discussion itself.

I Can See the Whole Room and There's Nobody In It! 1961
Oil and graphite on canvas. 48 x 48 inches / 122 x 122 cm
Private Collection

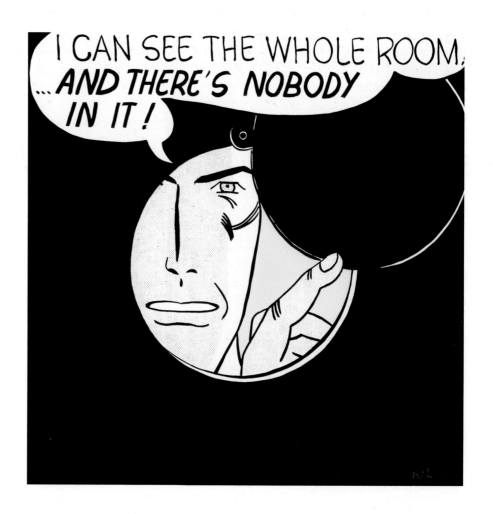

17

VII

One can view all of Lichtenstein's oeuvre in the light of the philosophical matrix formed by Hoyt Sherman's experiments – which does not mean that everything Lichtenstein did grew out of Sherman's paradigm: that would be to grant even a mentor too much. What I mean by matrix is the pattern that Sherman's experiments rendered visible – a pattern which, as mentioned before, extended the scope of the picture as a medium in two different directions.

On the one hand, the picture has the character of something that concentrates a flow or a flash into an image. This involves a belief that the image can be a revolt or intervention against the temporality that constantly obliterates what *is* in order to make room for what is to *come*. Thus the picture as a medium fixes something: a subject, an event or the attention of the viewer.

On the other hand, the *conditions* of image formation reveal that the continuum from which the senses draw their images can form images in all directions; and that the detached subject therefore does not exist, but in fact is to be understood as bodily vision tied to its location in time and space – and thus subject to the very relativity that one is trying to exorcize with one's unificatory gestures.

The two aspects belong together, respectively as the conditions of, and a challenge to, image-making – and Lichtenstein, as a classic iconoclast, positioned his practice in the field between these two poles. He painted pictures that are about the powerlessness of the image faced with the fullness or intensity that could have been the subject, and he painted pictures whose visual communicative impact there is no mistaking – but which offer us no edifying material to allay the iconoclastic suspicion that the important statements that can be made about first and last things cannot be made in a picture. While Philip Guston did not hesitate to let the finger of God draw a line in the dust as a reminder to the painter, Lichtenstein could take this no further than the shining star in Padre Pio.

VIII

With this point of departure – situated provocatively between the opposing notions of the power and powerlessness of the picture – we can pin down Lichtenstein's typology as a range of images that deal respectively with what the picture *cannot* do, and what it apparently *does* do.

To this area belongs a long succession of works which, both in terms of motive and theme, play through a kind of poetics of absence – despite the apparent insistent presence of the subject. It is a characteristic of Lichtenstein's art that one can almost gather these works into a catalogue of possible articulations, or rather typologies.

The pictures of girls are the best example – they span a wide typological horizon, but regarded as a whole, as a series, they appear as variations on the same theme: an emotive response to an external condition which the picture itself does not contain. Lichtenstein almost always avoids the moment of emotional climax in these pictures – they are always either about the naively prospective gaze of anticipation or about post-coital melancholy.

As regards the anticipation, the text in his speech bubbles is attached to the specific image as a visual response to what in stylistics is called *aposiopesis* – the figure which through tentative omission intensifies presence – "It's ... it's not an engagement ring. Is it?" Or the anticipation is there as a dreamy gaze over at the alarm clock – as in *Blonde Waiting*, 1964 – as if the very anticipation could transcend time – although if anything is dependent on time it is anticipation, for if time came to a halt things wouldn't look too good for the anticipator.

Common to the anticipation pictures is their dependence on a narrative schema which seems to swirl like concentric circles around the individual picture. Hilton Kramer was right when he wrote: "Only talk can effect the act of imaginative synthesis which the art itself fails to effect" – although he probably meant something quite different. This is a narrativity that the viewer cannot avoid. We are drawn into some statement by these pictures – it is not unlike the pornographic gaze, not *at* the model, but that comes

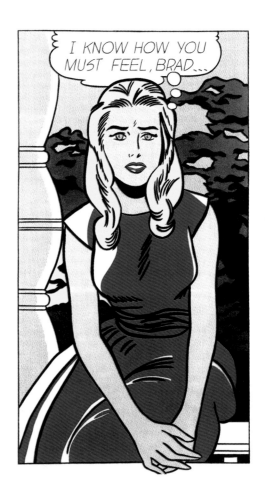

I know how you must feel, Brad... 1963
Oil on canvas. 66 1/2 x 37 3/4 inches / 168 x 96 cm
Neue Galerie, Aachen

from the model, that flows towards the user, since in combination with the immanent availability of the model it says "It's you I want!"

And so it is with Lichtenstein. I may not be Brad or Darling – *Good Morning... Darling*, 1964 – but I am the key to the picture's further expression of content. That is, if I am not simply a voyeur – which would only be a triangulation that would further complicate the relationship, even if in a very clear direction.

Only in a very small number of Lichtenstein's pictures of girls is the narratological gaze toned down; but then it is toned down in favour of an even more fundamental gaze, the typological gaze – in parodic versions of pathos formulae. There are close-up studies of melodramatic behaviour like *Frightened Girl* and *Happy Tears*, both from 1964, but even here the narrative horizon is close at hand: the frightened girl is clearly afraid of something outside the picture – shadows are descending over her – while the happy girl radiates relief over something or someone that is no longer – or perhaps precisely *is* – out of the picture.

In other words, Lichtenstein in all these anticipation pictures consistently paints up to the margin of a scene where something is happening, something that the picture has precluded itself from showing. That means two things. In the first place it involves the viewer in an interplay with the imaginary scenario. In the second it is a statement about the artistic image as such: that as a medium it is not only dependent on extrapictorial conditions. It also falls short of any claim that it can constitute an autonomous world.

In contrast to this theme of anticipation, we find what I will call the 'post-coital perdition' pictures. The star witness here is of course *Drowning Girl* from 1963, whose drama may seem to be at its climax, but is nevertheless past its peak. *Drowning Girl*'s source material is well known, so we need do no more than mention here how Lichtenstein has once more composed the picture by means of a number of clear choices and cuts, distinct from any scene in the comic strip. The picture is Lichtenstein's finest formulation of a counter-image to the many explosions in his universe – for this is maelstrom, implosion *par excellence*. The girl is sinking into the depths, completely

Blonde Waiting. 1964
Oil and Magna on canvas
48 x 48 inches / 122 x 122 cm
Collection Larry Gagosian, New York

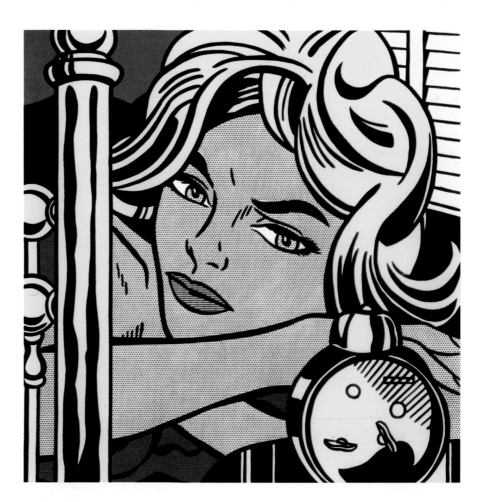

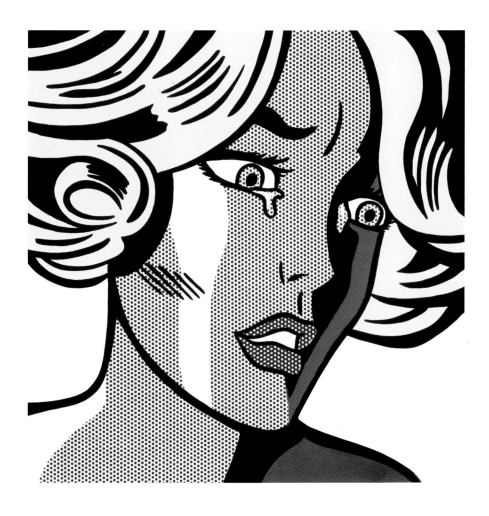

Frightened Girl. 1964
Oil on canvas. 48 x 48 inches / 122 x 136 cm
Collection Irving Blum, New York

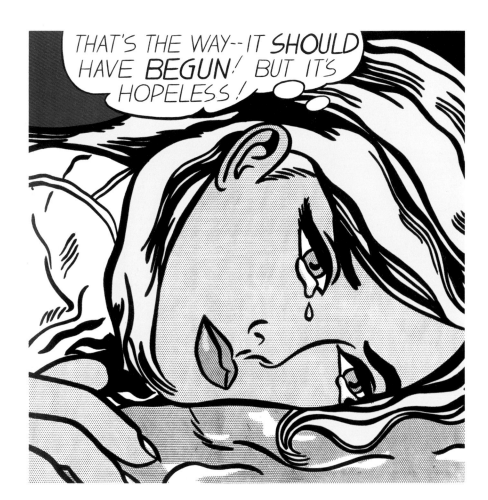

Hopeless. 1963
Oil on canvas. 44 x 44 inches / 112 x 112 cm
Private Collection

resigned, although her resignation is rooted in pride: rather die than give in to Brad. Although she is lying in water up to her neck, almost under one of the Hokusai-like waves, the tears are drawn with classic Lichtensteinian waxy fullness – popcorn tears – and you can assume they are important as a signal, for they can surely have no naturalistic justification in this scene of all-enveloping water.

Most of all, these tears – like so many other women's tears in Lichtenstein's work – are like the residue of the pornographic cum-shot, thus confirming the post-coital melancholy. *Drowning Girl* is as far as I know the only picture of a girl whose mouth is open beyond an unmarked white wall of teeth – one could see this vaginal detail as important to the pornographic aura of the scene.

The actual picture space is organized with a bizarre linkage of depth and surface. Lichtenstein has created an indeterminate space where the water runs around in a turbine-like wave form, but at the same time seems to stand still at the centre. Perhaps it is really a washing machine she is lying in!? The sense of glass in front of her, in front of the picture, is hard to ignore – and of course we know the whirlpool from the less sublime subject, *Washing Machine* from 1961, where spermatozoa perform an Aubrey Beardsley-like arabesque around a phallic centre. That these fluid forms – teardrops and whirlpools – are all precursor forms for the brushstrokes goes (almost) without saying.

With these images of anticipation and perdition the origin of the picture is visibly located outside the picture. As mentioned earlier, this can be interpreted in two ways: as an acknowledgement of the dependence of pictures on the outside world, and – by extension – as a critique of the autonomy of art and of the related fetishism that traditionally is associated with the generation that preceded Lichtenstein, the Abstract Expressionists. To sum up, one can say – to revert theoretically to Lessing's classic Laocoon discussion (Lichtenstein has of course painted the very theme in *Laocoon*, 1988) – that the narrative (or as we must insist, the narratological) pictures explore the boundaries of what the picture can contain, and that these boundaries then in turn become the picture's communicative interface with the viewer.

Drowning Girl 1963
Oil and synthetic polymer paint on canvas
67 5/8 x 66 3/4 inches / 172 x 170 cm
The Museum of Modern Art, New York,
Philip Johnson Fund and gift of
Mr. And Mrs. Bagley Wright

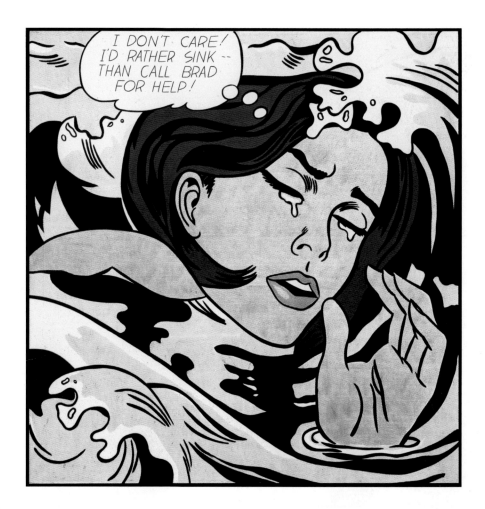

IX

Thus the narratological pictures are about a capturable instant that is only capturable because it is supplemented on both sides by the co-narrating viewer's reconstruction of a past and construction of a future. However, yet another kind of instant is at play in Lichtenstein, and it is almost a category in its own right: the explosion.

What is an explosion really? Fundamentally, it is a violent chemical increase in volume. The crucial dimension, though, is its temporality – the suddenness with which the increase occurs. An explosion is a curve that snaps, a mould that bursts. When something explodes, its original form is destroyed. Thus it is not time that wears it down but the absence of time, its cessation. Explosions are anti-history, although as apocalyptic moments they are sometimes assumed to be driving forces in history.

Roy Lichtenstein is mad about explosions! No doubt about it. In his workbooks you can see them as independent objects of study, cut out of the comic books – and of course they play a natural role in his many war pictures. In the major work *Whaam!*, 1963, the explosive theme is still kept within a kind of reduced narrative schema – we see the pilot firing the missile, and we see the enemy plane at the moment of annihilation, but we do not see the missile itself. *Whaam!* is therefore both a picture of an explosion and a suggestive image of an *implosion*, that is the implosion of the picture itself. So if the explosion is in general the collapse of representativity, then Lichtenstein's representation of this is an intensification of the power of the picture, a theme he later perfected in his three-dimensional representations of explosions, where the image becomes sculpture.

In Lichtenstein's explosions, presence and absence are two sides of the same thing. Explosions sever the connection between image and narrative, only to unite them again as pure manifestation. For that reason he did not limit the use of the explosion to the war pictures, but spread them through the oeuvre as a formula for the non-representable to which he constantly reverted. *Popeye* is one example mentioned before: the picture shows an explosive punch – Popeye versus Bluto – but the point of contact is empty. The explosive instant is the black hole of the picture, with stars strewn around it.

In other words, we see the effect, not the actual effective force. Or take the self-portrait – *Drawing for Coup de Chapeau (Self portrait)*, 1995 – an invisible force only visible from its comet-tail, with the hovering hat and glasses as the rudimentary attributes of the person depicted; the face itself is a vibrating point blank inscribed in

Comic book source material

Sketch for Explosion (The New Fall of America). (1992)
Graphite on paper
6 5/8 x 5 inches / 16.8 x 12.7 cm

Comic book source material

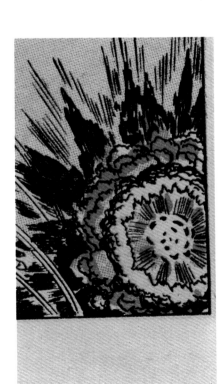

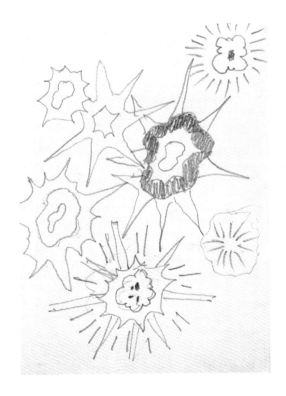

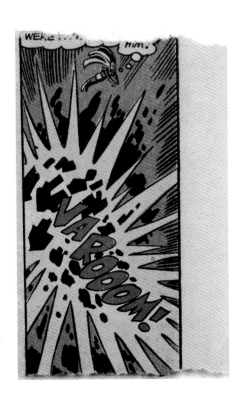

83.
Drawing for "Coup de Chapeau
(Self Portrait)". 1995
Private Collection

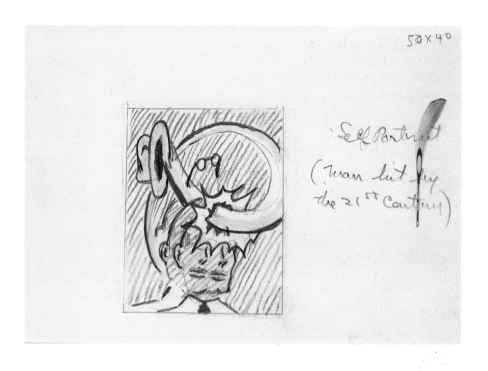

Pop! – drawing. 1966
Cut and pasted printed paper and felt pen
28 1/2 x 22 inches / 72.4 x 55.9 cm
Private Collection

Flatten...Sandfleas! 1962
Oil and Magna on canvas
34 x 44 inches / 86 x 112 cm

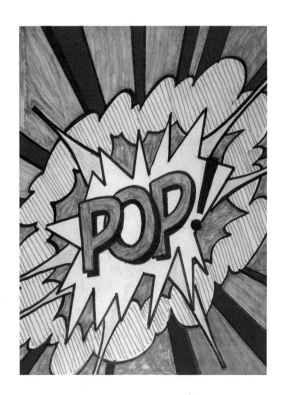

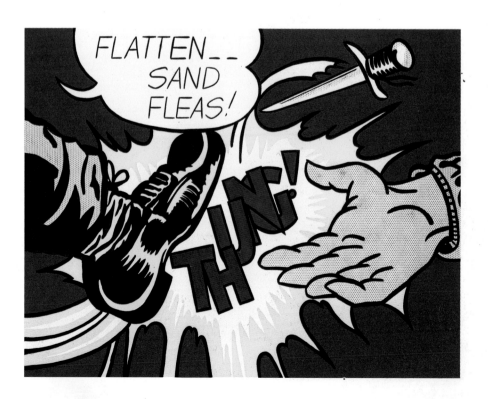

equal proportions of energy and silent-movie gimmickry – Lichtenstein has written "Man hit by the 21st Century" on the drawing. He could equally have written "Man hit by a brushstroke"! The drawing is almost like a remake of *Sweet Dreams Baby!*, a screen print from 1965, which in turn takes up the thread from the painting *Flatten ... Sandfleas* from 1962. The explosive markers develop from the stars in *Popeye* through "POW!" and "THUNG!" and "WHAAM!" to purely pictorially-marked detonations of energy.

X

It is no wonder that the explosion becomes such a dominant theme for Lichtenstein, if we remember that his works are about pinning down the performative power of images. The explosion is the trademark reduced *ad absurdum.* It is the direct, instant pictorial effect subsumed into the aesthetic space of destruction, and Lichtenstein's explosions in other words offer the same as his many early crystal-clear pictures did: the unmistakable image. What you see is what you see. A hot dog, a standing rib, a radio with a leather strap, a cup of coffee.

Yet the unmistakability of these pictures is constantly threatened by our familiarity with the subject, which becomes a potentially anecdotal counterpoint to the iconic potency of the motif. We can start to elaborate a narrative with these pictures, just as we do as soon as Brad & co. make their appearance. With the explosions, the anecdotal comes to a halt – even when they are embedded in war scenes. It is therefore this very halt, the cessation of narrative, that the explosions dramatize. The next – I am tempted to say the next natural – step is therefore the brushstrokes.

Normally Lichtenstein's brushstroke paintings are viewed as inextricably bound up with an art-historical situation, his showdown with the Abstract Expressionist generation. They are read as a deconstruction of the idea of the brushstroke as special, intimate evidence of the artist's personality – Lichtenstein transforming gestural flow and materiality into a kind of graphic technique (as a curious footnote, however, Lichtenstein had to make a real brushstroke on acetate and then project it onto the canvas, because it was simply not possible for him to 'mime' a brushstroke by drawing it).

It is undoubtedly true that Lichtenstein's brushstroke paintings can be read as part of this conflict; one just has to make sure that one reads them far enough in, so to speak. It is not enough to see the brushstroke paintings as superficial parodies of

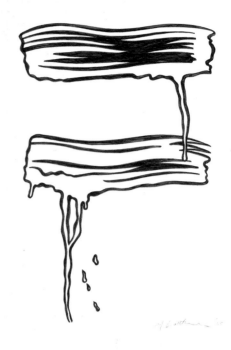

70.
Brushstroke studies. 1965
Private Collection

81.
Brushstroke Face. 1987
Private Collection

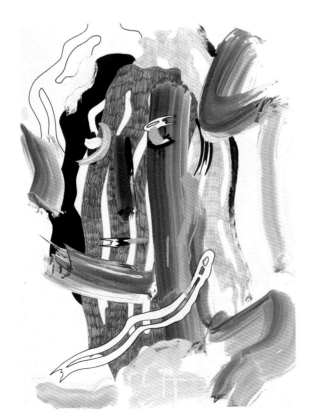

abstract painting; they are much more about the issues in Lichtenstein's own art that I am trying to outline here.

Lichtenstein's brushstrokes are explosions in slow motion. Whereas the explosion's sudden release of energy conceals its effective energy source, the brushstrokes extend the explosive process, stretch it out, give it a kind of development – but on the other hand involve no narrative whatsoever. The brushstrokes thus locate themselves at a fascinating point between the explosion and the speech bubble – and one cannot help noticing how Lichtenstein, in the drips accompanying the individual strokes, mimics the graphic psychology of the speech bubble – line as a marker of mood. As early as the drawing *Airplane* from 1961 the object (the plane) is set against a background (a cloud), which has a kind of vibrancy. Bernice Rose may be right in saying of this work: "Nor does the drawing show any artistic temperament"; but she is hardly right in saying that it is "emotionally neutral".[5]

Lichtenstein was a master of the use of the marginal narrative values inherent in the shape of the speech bubble – a theme he also carried over into the brushstroke paintings – expressed most clearly in *Yellow Brushstroke I*, 1965, which quite simply looks like a kind of speech bubble, a *Cold Shoulder* where only the cold is left.

XI

Lichtenstein's brushstroke is first and foremost gestural[6] – and it is partly in this light that we should see his famous *Sponge* from 1962 as a symbolic precursor – it is a blackboard being wiped clean, but it is still a hand that runs the show. Earlier in his life as a painter – at the end of the 1950s – he had adopted the brushstroke as a category in a number of pictures, for example *Variations #7*, 1959, where the tonalities in the individual stroke became a kind of candy-striping, an attempt at expurgating the material micro-life of the painting – its microbial swarm of colours in the hand-painted texture. In the hardcore brushstroke paintings of the 1960s the tonality was transformed into a simple but effective interplay of light (colour) and shade (black), which mimed the impasto of the loaded painterly brushstroke.

These paintings are pictures of brushstrokes – just as his subjects are pictures of subjects. They reach both out of and into Lichtenstein's work: externally they are to do with a certain painterly convention, internally – and once more with model clarity – they not only manifest an investigation of painting as such, but act as a response to the

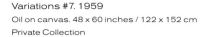

Variations #7. 1959
Oil on canvas. 48 x 60 inches / 122 x 152 cm
Private Collection

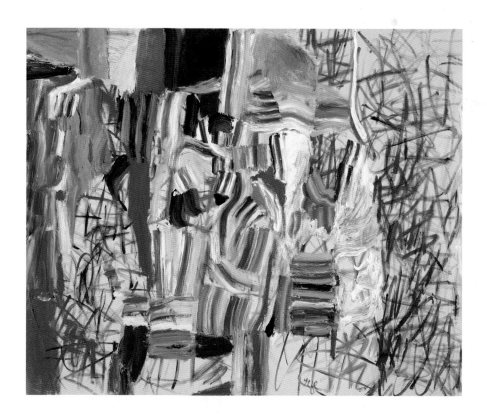

challenge Lichtenstein had set himself: to capture the picture-as-picture in a confrontation with almost any kind of subject matter. The brushstroke is just another kind of subject matter in the long list from Donald Duck and roller skates to mirrors, Mondrians and Matisses.

But one should not confuse subject matter with content here; the content is actually somewhat different. The content of the brushstroke paintings is the ongoing examination of the relationship in the paintings between narrative, time and the moment, and the ongoing examination of the role of the beholder, the deconstruct of the authentic relationship between me and the paintings.

The brushstroke paintings are a new version of the iconic object paintings. The object paintings invite you into the realm of easy recognition, but tell you nothing. The brushstroke is the next step in this examination of visual communication on behalf of painting, the *mise-en-scène* of painting *par excellence*. We can still identify the subject matter, but what we identify is actually nothing. And this nothing is not even a representation of something (hidden) – which is precisely the true point of Lichtenstein's critique of the painterly tradition. The only thing we can do is contemplate, unfold time along the lines of the brushstroke. That gets us nowhere – the sublime may be now, but Lichtenstein has successfully turned the apocalyptic zip into a kind of pastoral.

XII

If the brushstroke paintings are the stretching-out of an event so that it becomes visible solely as a kind of rhetoric, as a device, a model, a meta-statement (but still sensually present), then Lichtenstein's landscapes can be understood in similar terms. His landscape paintings include both early pop-stylized versions of specific scenes from comic strips and commercial tourist posters – from sunsets to Greek temples – and the later Chinese views.

Of course Lichtenstein was once more drawing on the tradition of art history, but unlike his paraphrases of Mondrian and Monet, for example, he was not repainting specific landscape paintings; it was the 'category' of landscape painting itself that interested him. Just as Lichtenstein's critique of Abstract Expressionism consisted of transforming a space of experience into a category, a rhetorical device – which in turn explains why Surrealism was pure serendipity for him, for already here this transformation was seminal to the very project of the artists – his landscape paintings too are a kind of expulsion of the human from art.

Romantic landscape painting basically deals with harmonies and discords between nature and man – with the sublime and the picturesque as opposite poles. But Lichtenstein expunged all this. There may be some archaeological remains – a piece of broken column *à la* de Chirico – but otherwise the scene is usually empty. Just as Lichtenstein's brushstrokes manifest little more than pure gesture, his landscapes are simply vacancies – resonance chambers for emptiness. Not even Friedrich's figures with their backs to us are allowed in – and there is a reason for this.

The reason is that Lichtenstein's landscapes are a kind of pure space where the classic conflict between man and nature has been overcome. The landscapes are problem-free – for the most part they are precisely pastoral scenes without time, narrative or event. And yet time has not been completely removed. What the brushstrokes did with time – unfolded it modestly *as if in a now*, but still only *as if* – the landscapes do by virtue of their spatial distribution. They are undramatic – even when the towering cumulus clouds throng.

But there is one thing Lichtenstein learned from Friedrich: to abandon the form of the 'stage' and keep the panorama open at the sides. But while this opens up the world for Friedrich and makes it into a disquieting *outer space*, the effect in Lichtenstein's landscapes is more limited. Here it is all about the landscape as a kind of passage; the feeling one associates with most of Lichtenstein's landscapes is not that of the gaze that loses itself in the vanishing-point of vast space, but rather of the panning shot. We pass sideways through the picture, as if we were reading it – or as if it were an ornament! Or – why not? – an entablature.

This is clearest in pictures like *Yellow Sky*, 1966, where the whole painting looks like an electrocardiogram of the landscape; but in the more voluminous landscapes like *Sussex*, 1964, there is still a pulse that undulates through the picture rather than closing it off as a subject. Even the Chinese landscapes, which introduce residually figurative entities at the edge of the scene, maintain an open space where the feeling of passage is stronger than the feeling of abiding presence. In several of these landscapes Lichtenstein has, for example, run a shadow through the picture which also functions as kind of transient rhythm.

In other words the landscapes are an unassuming stretch of time, but it is no longer narrative time. As a category in Lichtenstein's universe it is close to both the explosion's and the brushstroke's challenge to temporality – and if we go back for a brief moment to *Whaam!*, it is significant that, under the wing of the attacking plane, we see the finest of cloud landscapes with a Morris Louis-like signature drawn through it. The motif was used as the front cover of the catalogue for the Tate Gallery's Roy Lichtenstein exhibition in 1968. It communicates nothing of *Whaam!*'s gestural and sonic energy, but does show a pastoral parenthesis amidst the explosiveness – and is thus fully compatible with it.

The landscapes manifest a kind of time that is no longer tied to reading, a more diffuse sense of time associated deep down with a *specific* kind of reading – that is, the reading of the ornament. They give a hint that Lichtenstein's art is moving towards this, towards the ornament's remarkable reconciliation of time and repetition, of space and line.

XIII

Up to now I have tried to identify Roy Lichtenstein's pictures as an ongoing investigation of the picture itself, asking "What do paintings do?"

Lichtenstein's interest in the image is identical to his interest in painting – the picture as art is still his goal. In that respect Lichtenstein is a classical artist – he has no intention of negating art or deconstructing painting. Quite the contrary, I would say: he

Cover from the Tate Gallery catalogue
for the exhibition *Roy Lichtenstein*,
6 January – 4 February 1968.
Detail from Whaam! 1963 (cat. no. 19)
Design Michael Brawne

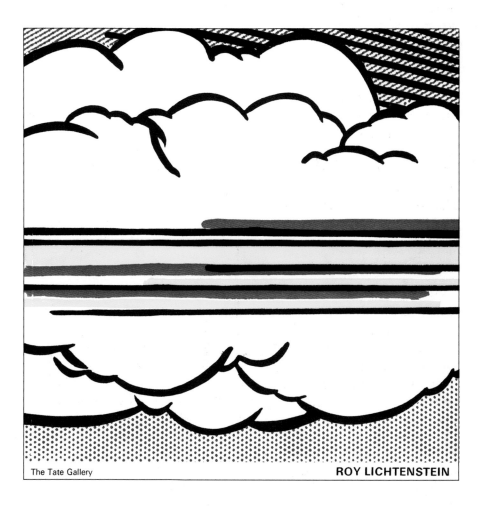

tries, if not to reconstruct it, at least to construct it by allowing it to face contemporary challenges.

Lichtenstein's critical approach to painting as an established field thus results in a long succession of paintings that rely on a distinction between the subject matter and the content of the art work. This is a strategy that recalls what Umberto Eco, in a literary context, has called 'dual coding', where the artist plays on a recognition at the surface and uses this recognition to initiate something (else) elsewhere in the work. Lichtenstein is of course not as *specifically* interested in bathrooms, English landscapes, kitchen fittings, sneakers and stretchers as he is in the reflections on painting prompted by these objects or categories when they are transferred into the space of visual art.

However, I have also suggested that his choices of subject matter cannot be described as arbitrary, and that it is Lichtenstein's merit that he so to speak qualifies his subject matter or lets it qualify the content of the picture.

Thus, the subject matter is not irrelevant to the content of Roy Lichtenstein's work. Just as Cézanne, Picasso, Mondrian and Monet are singled out for their affinity with a complex of artistic problems, which Lichtenstein shares[7], *Washing Machine* is related to *Drowning Girl*, which is related to the mixture of exorcism and perdition expressed by the brushstroke paintings. The red *Painting*, 1965, whose title can both be a noun and a gerund, interestingly enough has its source in a comic strip where it *is* an exorcism – an obliteration of the painting itself: a so-called overpainting.

In the same way the war scenes, with their many explosions, and the tragic blondes, also serve, *by virtue of* their subject matter, to stage a specific content: the investigation of the picture's narratology, its performative power and the limits of that power, its relationship with the viewer as a representation of time and space.

I have attempted to suggest how Lichtenstein, despite his figurativeness (or because of it) insists, first, that the artistic picture does something that other pictures do not – whether it is unification or an ironic critique of the attempt to do so; second, that the precondition of this is a societal situation where the image plays a greater role than before, and therefore helps to stylize human experience; third, how this means that art too has its version of what trademarks are to industry; and fourth, that this very branding activity involves its own version of the performative power of the artistic image; and – finally – that Lichtenstein himself, in his own oeuvre, both investigates this performative power, its limits and its possibilities, and at the same time tries himself to practice it through a sharpening of his artistic idiom, which first and foremost intends to phase out narrative temporality as a horizon for the picture.

Presumably few would disagree that Roy Lichtenstein's pictures have performative power. At an uncontroversial level, this means that the artist's devices and composition, his use of colour and motif, generate pictures that have a high degree of recognizability and unmistakability – the latter evident not least from the way the advertising industry has retained and recycled Lichtenstein's style, which has thus come full circle – and an immediate effect. Lichtenstein is in other words a master of the surface, which is not the same as being master of the superficial or even a superficial master …

Being able to intensify the performative power of the picture in this way is not a matter of course: the philosopher Hegel noted long ago that the magical power of visual art (in his case as a stimulus to religious veneration) had lost its hold on nineteenth-century man – the image of the Madonna no longer had the effect it once had. So, what religion (and visual art) had to give up – the physical impact of the image – others took over, in debased modes of the absolute spirit: advertising and the pornographic industry.

The pornographic *in abstracto* can be found in Lichtenstein in his total stylization, just as the advertising industry's fascination with the object recurs everywhere. But it is pornography without sex and it is advertising without names. The brand names have disappeared and the sexual has been transformed into cynical sentimentality at the most. The investigations, the ongoing analysis of the performative power of the image, persist. Without reservations. And not without inspiration from those fields in which they are still exploited as something other than art.

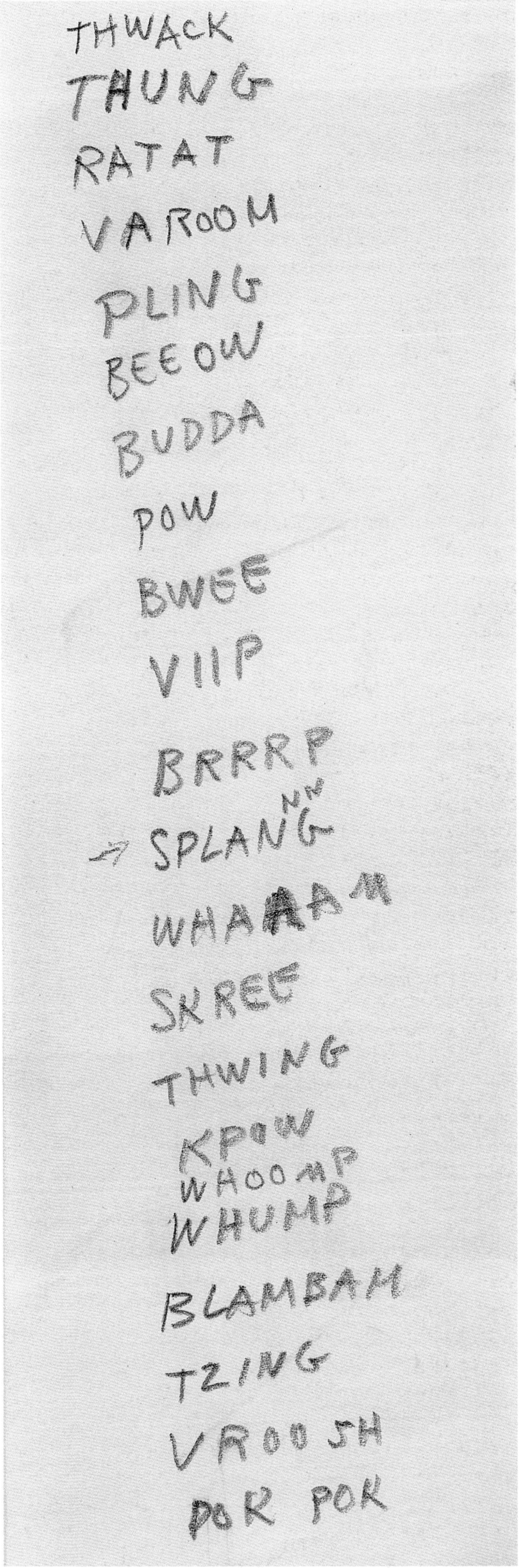

THWACK
THUNG
RATAT
VAROOM
PLING
BEEOW
BUDDA
POW
BWEE
VIIP

BRRRP
→ SPLANG^{NN}
WHAAAM
SKREE
THWING
KPOW
WHOOMP
WHUMP

BLAMBAM
TZING
VROOSH
POR POK

Hand Written Word List, n.d.
Graphite on paper
8 1/2 x 3 inches / 21.6 x 7.6 cm
Private Collection

XIV

Lichtenstein's analytical scrutiny of the transmission from image to art triggers off a paradoxical linkage between figurativity and timelessness in his own oeuvre. With the comic strip paintings he initiates his narratological trick, which consistently permits the viewer to unfold mentally the residue of time in the work – the framework that surrounds it – but then he phases out the temporality in a number of experiments; he proceeds from time to simultaneity. We have mentioned the category of 'explosions' as the most telling example of this; we could also have mentioned Lichtenstein's fondness for 'still life' – or his paraphrases of Picasso, Mondrian and others, which attempt to confirm these artworks as things that are no longer experienced in time and space but as existing categories – as 'a Picasso', 'a Mondrian', 'a Monet'. Second hand experience.

This intensification of the visual statement by distancing himself from its narrativity reaches its peak in Lichtenstein's brushstroke paintings and in his entablatures. These pictures – despite their abstraction, and like Lichtenstein's so-called 'abstract paintings' – are still figurative in a certain sense, I would claim. For they are figurative pictures of abstractions. And thus they still function as something readable – but now with a different time from the narrative invested in them. It takes a diffuse reading that does not follow the temporality we know from the literary schema – an experience of time that has more to do with passage through space, as in the landscapes, than a progress along the lines of the musical score.

In other words it is the time of the ornament, which is in principle endless – like in the circular *Tire*, 1962, which seems to be Lichtenstein's first ornament along with the Pollock-like *Composition I & II*, 1964 – and which therefore need not or cannot be read to the end. Here surface no longer stands in contrast to depth, just as instant and progression can no longer be separated. Lichtenstein, who throughout his life continued to be preoccupied with the idea of the picture as 'unification', as an extension of the studies of his youth with Hoyt Sherman, is close to achieving his goal here.

Simultaneity as an aesthetic ideal, finally, is something we find in the many emphatically contoured spaces that Lichtenstein also painted, besides the open landscapes. For Lichtenstein's *Interiors* and *Artist's Studio* paintings too have simultaneity as a hallmark. The only markers of the limits of simultaneity are the mirrors that make the space uncertain by virtue of their optical (not to be confused with realistic) illusions, but the uncertainty is far from reintroducing any narrative schema. On the contrary, it renders impossible that 'unification' which narrative or the viewer's unique identification of the space could bring about; it defers the synthesizing gaze or throws it back at the viewer. The pictorial elements can be strung together into a continuous chain of appropriations; they are staccato, or else they are the harmonious coexistence of the many perspectives – beyond time and space I was tempted to say; and thus they represent a 'unification' on another plane, the plane of the painting.

XV

Roy Lichtenstein's pictures – what are they, then? Mirrors, windows, doors or screens, behind which there is nothing?

Probably very few people would perceive Lichtenstein as an existentialist artist; that is, an artist who offers us human stories with which the viewer can empathize, or alternatively paintings which the artist himself has lived through. Although for much of the way the viewer plays along with the aid of his or her narrative supplementation, and although Lichtenstein has unmistakably had a hand in this game from first to last, the work remains as something that is not accessible in any true sense.

Lichtenstein's pictures are hard. They are precise, and they are consistent. There is no story within them – if they have a story to tell, it takes place on the margins of the space and time of the picture; and for that matter it is also *about* these margins. And that is in fact where we are, where *we* come into the picture.

So the stories are ours, but the picture will not exhaust them. It does what it can, and more, but in the final analysis, it remains a kind of blocking-off from what for Lichtenstein would be an unpleasant scenario, if reality were to coincide with its image, if reality were to be identical to our image of it. That does not mean that we do not need images to cope with reality – but it also means that we need reality in order to cope with images.

In other words, I view Lichtenstein in this respect as a moral artist; an artist who sharpens our sense of the extent to which existence is offered to us in model form – and of the extent to which it is necessary to recognize a model when we see one.

With Lichtenstein, Hoyt Sherman's training has been superseded by training in pattern recognition, or call it genre-consciousness, or rhetorical cultivation. Otherwise we could end up like Donald Duck, who thinks he has caught the world, but has only caught himself – in *Look Mickey*, 1961, a painting which in a parodic, embryonic form contains Lichtenstein's coupling of the idea of autonomy with self-reference – and besides that, *M-Maybe* Edvard Munch's *The Scream* taken to the point of absurdity with jetty and painterly whirlpool, Mickey with his hand not over his ears, but his mouth – comical perdition…

XVI

Lichtenstein himself spoke of his anti-sensibility as pivotal. He was at the same time fully aware that there is still sensibility even in this anti-sensibility. German philosophers with a penchant for hard words call this the *Unhintergehbarkeit* of the subject, meaning that one cannot escape the source of escaping, as one cannot deconstruct or criticize without still being there, present in the very gesture. Or in Lichtenstein's words: "I want my work to look programmed or impersonal, but I don't believe I'm being impersonal while I do it … We tend to confuse the style of the finished work with the methods in which it was done." We might say simply that Lichtenstein knew that art was art, which makes him a Classicist. On behalf of art. Unlike the Romantic Warhol. "I was an old-fashioned artist compared with him", Lichtenstein said.[8]

One could accuse Lichtenstein of many things, including being a modest man – in the Lichtenstein archives there are two interesting little lists, one listing the pathos formulae of popular culture, the onomatopoetics of the comic strip – *Pling, Bwee, Viip, Tzing, Pok Pok* – and another one listing around fifteen polite ways of responding positively – in real life.

In other words, he was an artist who stuck to the surface and contour line in his paintings throughout his life – irrespective of the fact that neither of them appears in reality as it does in his art. The contour does not encompass things like a line in our sensory perception, and the surface is only there from a very superficial point of view.

So pure and authentic inwardness is very hard to trace in Roy Lichtenstein's oeuvre – but then that is the point. And in precisely this we find his defence – in the analysis of outwardness, which reflects his dedication to the real as an important prerequisite for both understanding and coping with pictures. That is the point of his iconoclasm: that a lot would be lost if the picture, the image, art, had to account for everything.

"Hello!", says the girl in *Cold Shoulder*. It drips from the icicles of the speech bubble, but the girl herself – judging from her back – doesn't look especially chilly.

Who knows?

Knock! Knock!

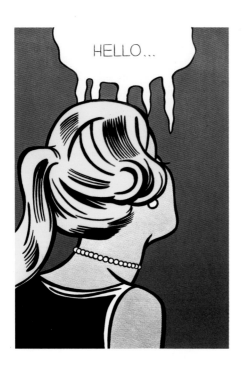

14.
Cold Shoulder. 1963
Collection Robert H. Halff

P.E. Tøjner has a PhD in Literature with a dissertation on Søren Kierkegaard. He has been a critic and an editor of a newspaper for many years, and written several books on art, philosophy, literature, architecture and design. In 2000 he was appointed director of Louisiana Museum of Modern Art.

1   Edgar Allan Poe, "The Raven", *Selected Writings*, Penguin, London, 1967
2   Cf. Marco Livingstone's *Pop Art,* London, 1991, p. 16
3   Cf. Diane Waldman, *Roy Lichtenstein,* New York, 1971, p. 11
4   My use of and account of Hoyt Sherman is based on Michael Lobel's excellent book *Image Duplicator,* New Haven & London, 2002.
5   Bernice Rose, *The Drawings of Roy Lichtenstein,* MoMA, New York, 1987, p. 16
6   Cf. Jack Cowart in *Roy Lichtenstein*, Fondation Beyeler, 1998
7   Cf. Diane Waldman, *Roy Lichtenstein,* New York, 1971, p. 11
8   Cf. Michael Lobel, *Image Duplicator,* New Haven & London, 2002, p. 20

Many thanks to Martin Caiger-Smith for his criticism and response, which has clarified several points – at least to the author himself.

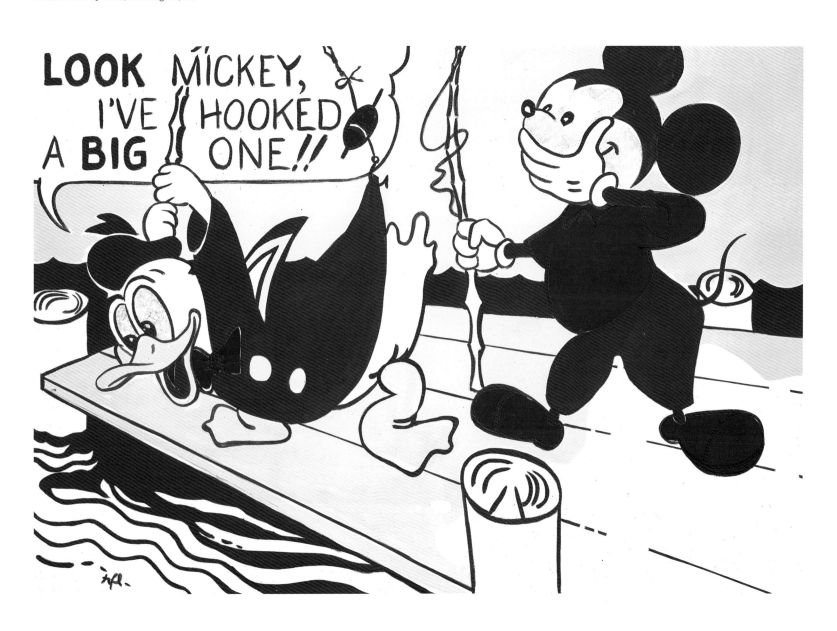

4.
Popeye. 1961
David Lichtenstein

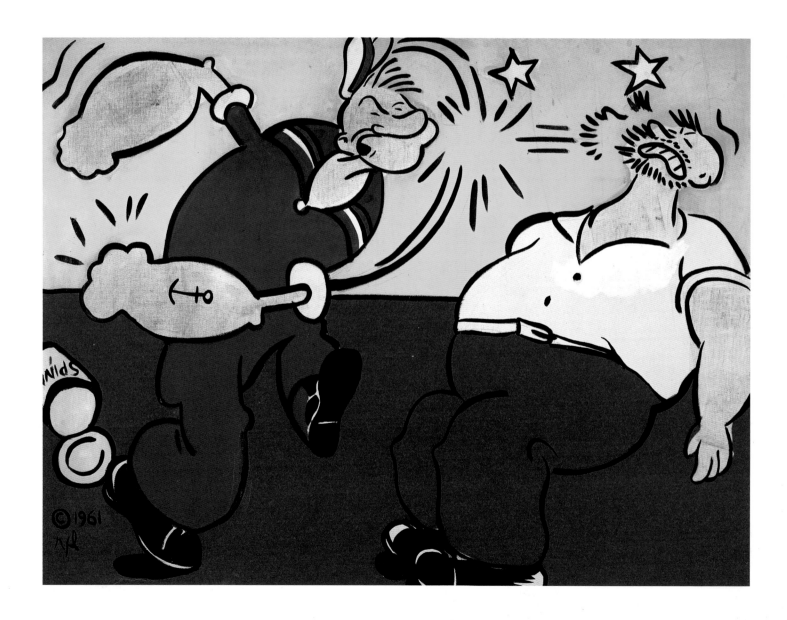

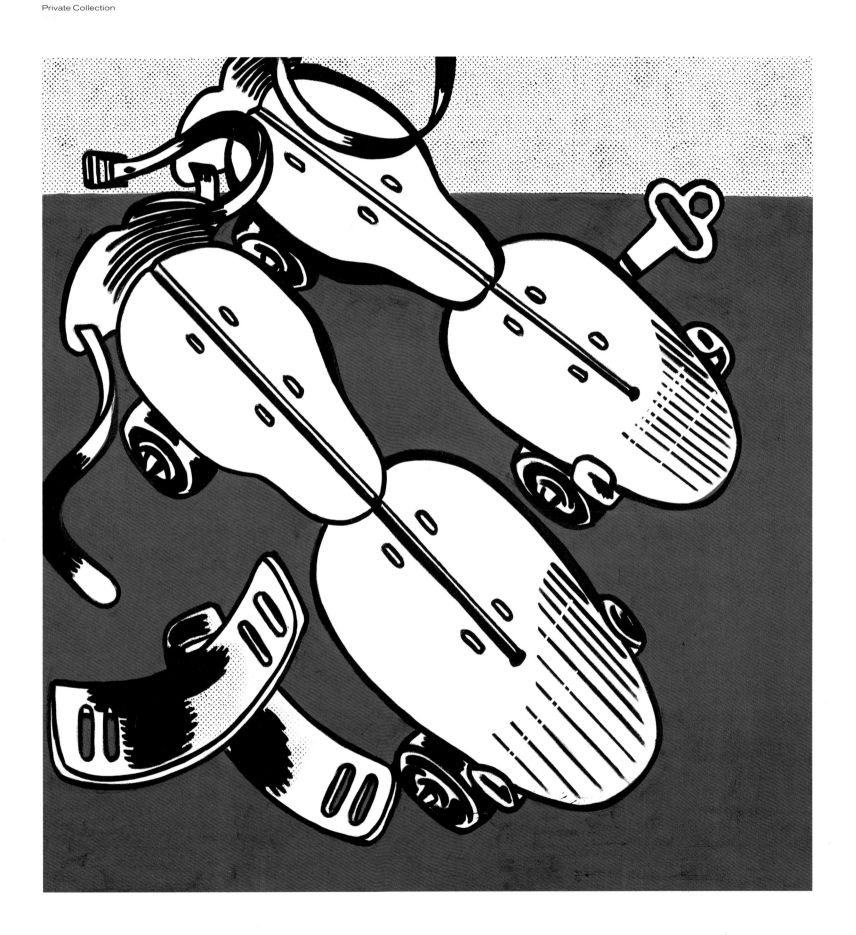

Cup of Coffee. 1961
Roy Lichtenstein Foundation Collection

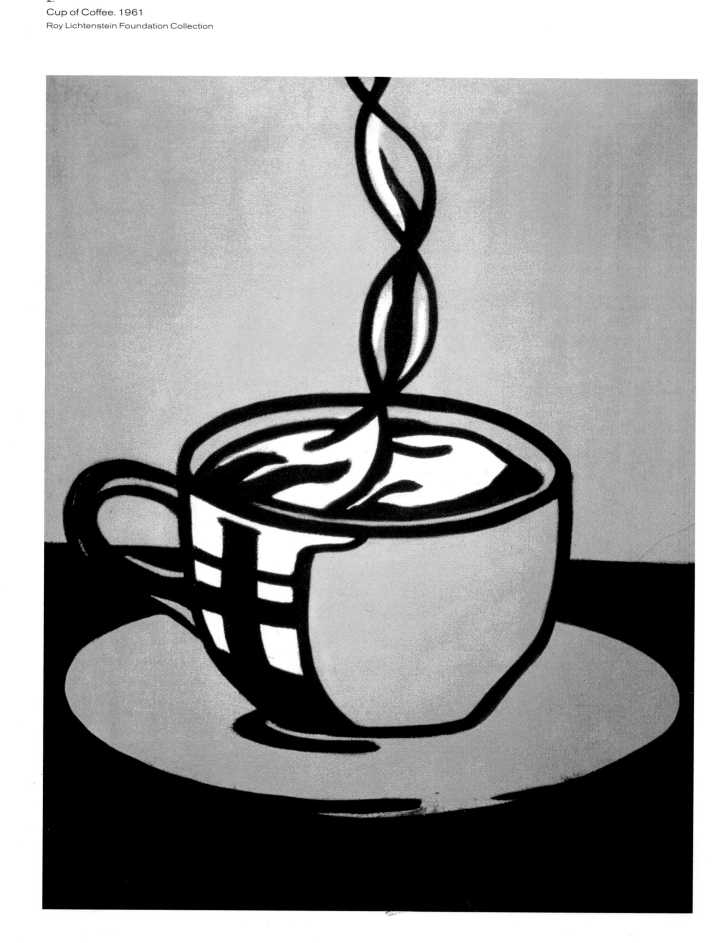

1.
Bathroom. 1961
Whitney Museum of American Art, New York

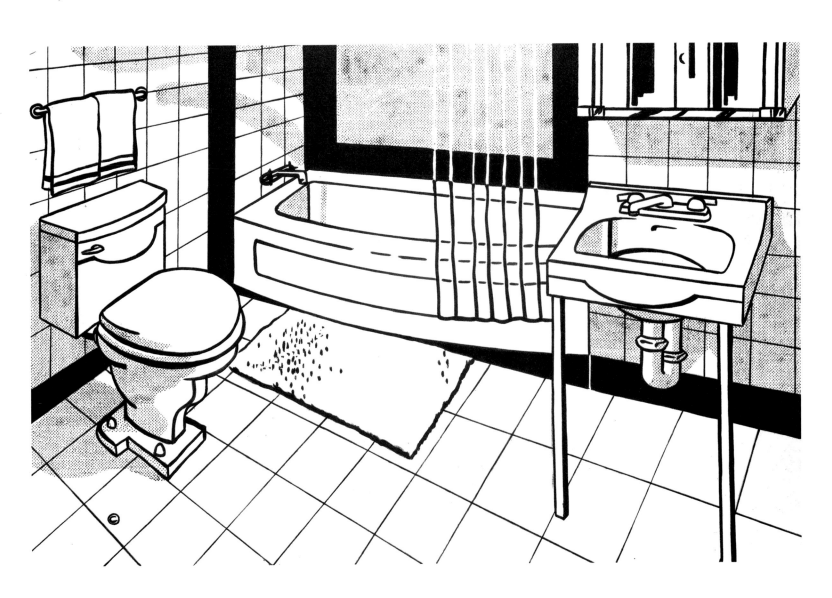

7.
Washing Machine. 1961
Yale University Art Gallery

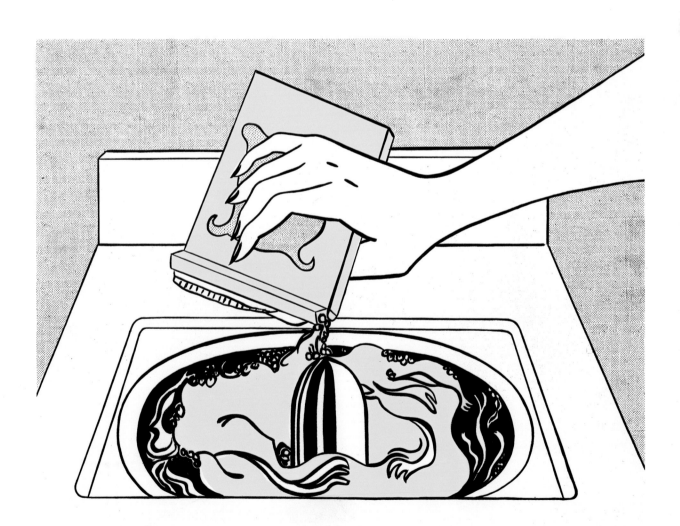

9.
Desk Calendar. 1962
The Museum of Contemporary Art, Los Angeles.
The Panza Collection

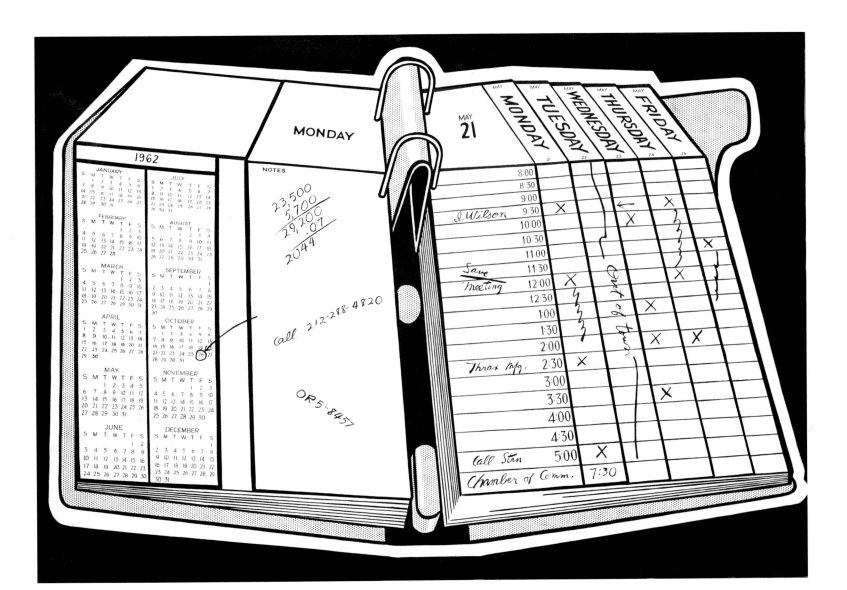

12.
Standing Rib. 1962
The Museum of Contemporary Art, Los Angeles.
The Panza Collection

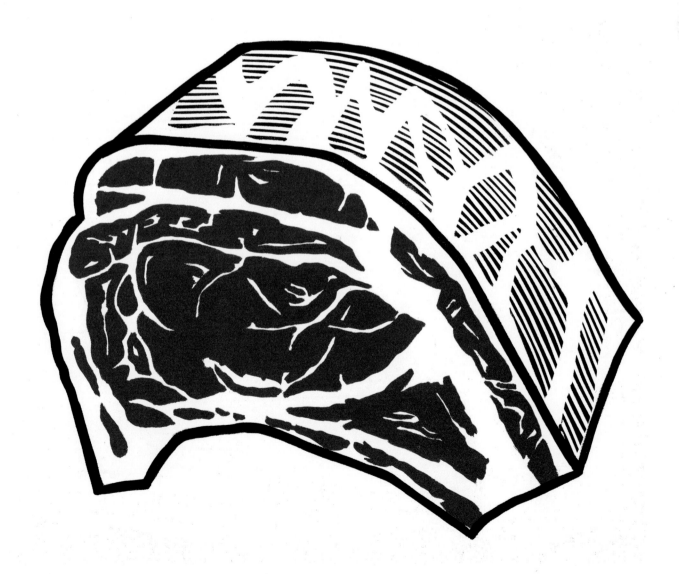

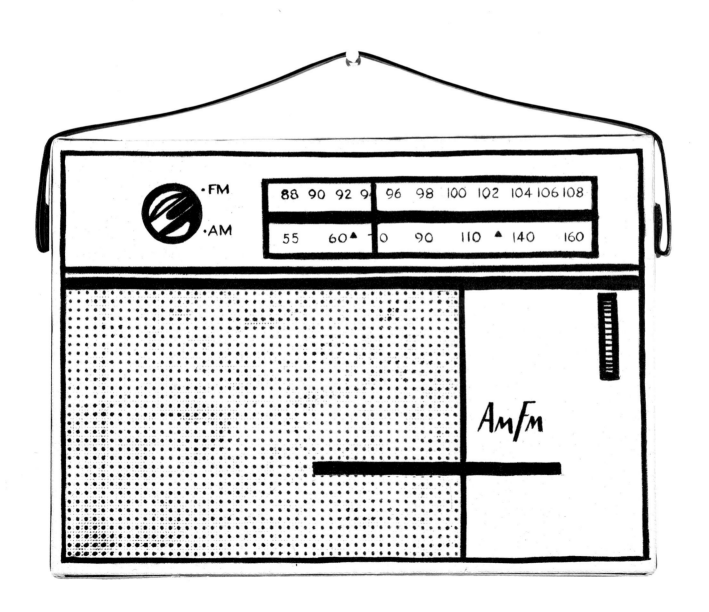

10.
Golf Ball. 1962
Private Collection

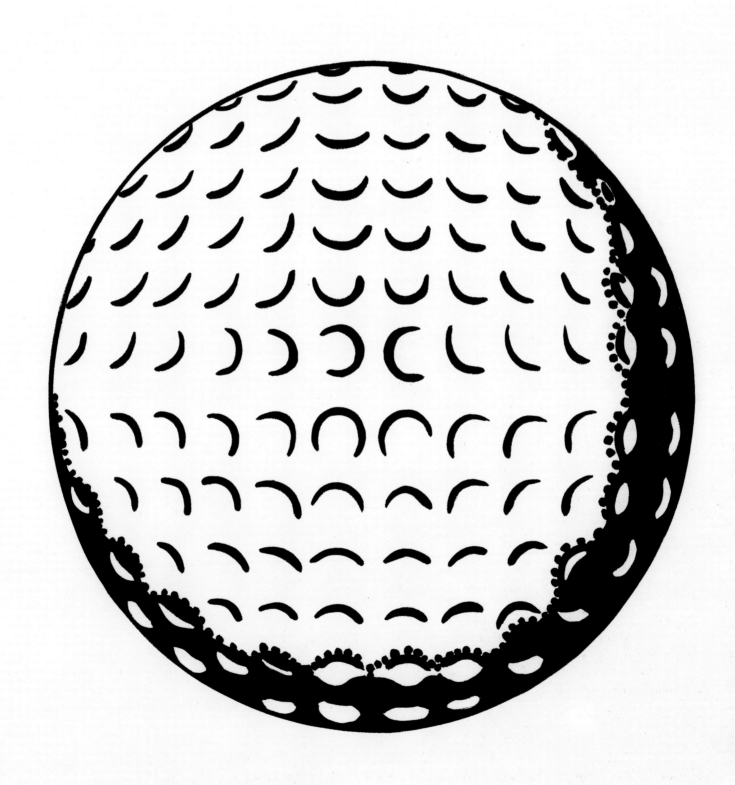

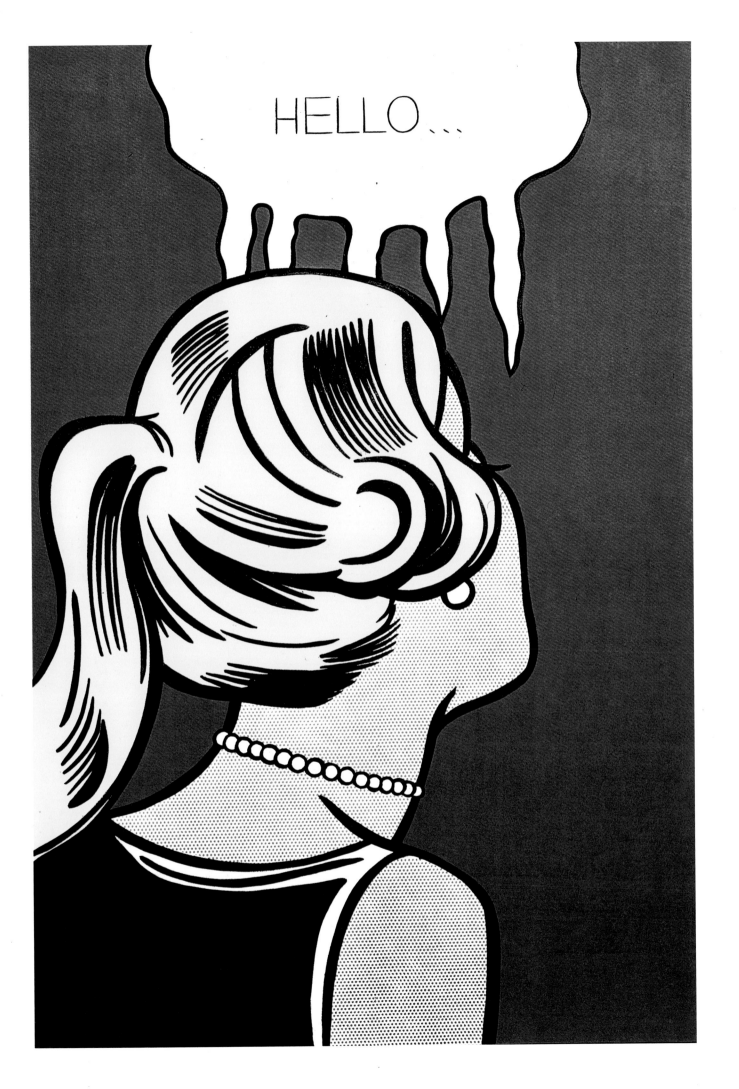

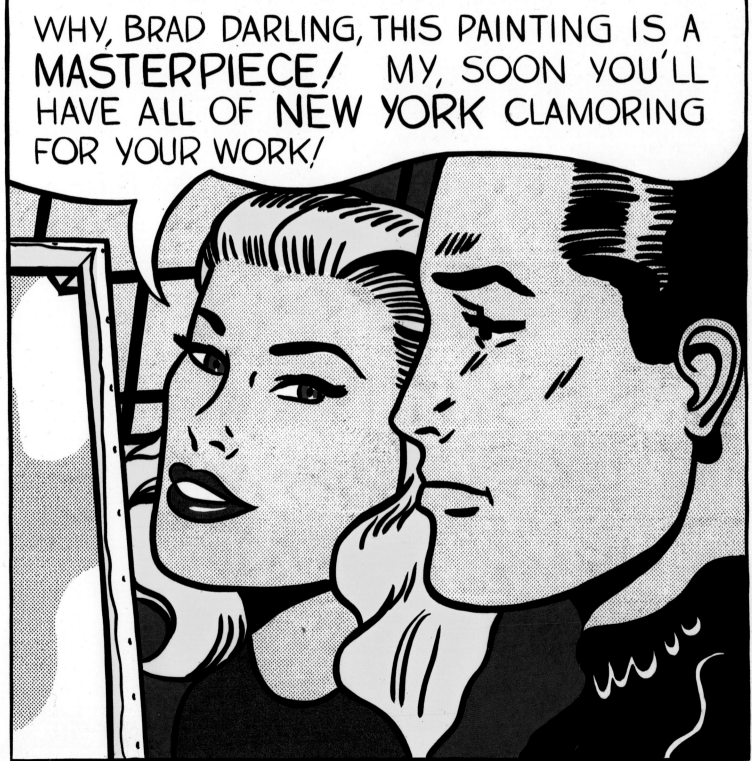

13.
Ball of Twine. 1963
Courtesy The Brant Foundation, Greenwich, Connecticut, USA

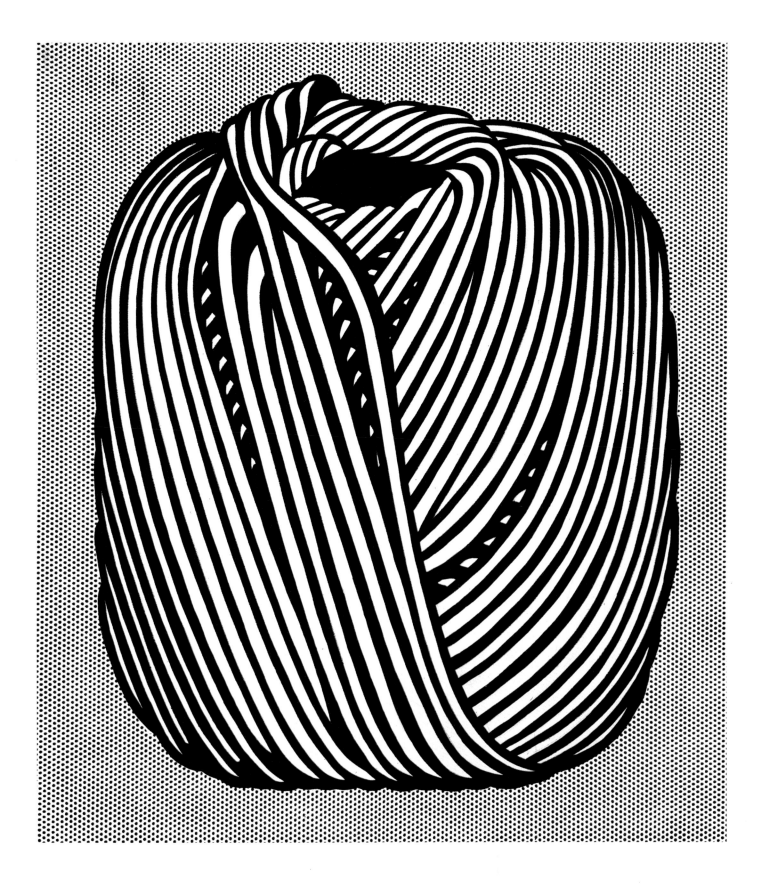

15.
Half Face with Collar. 1963
Collection Gian Enzo Sperone, New York

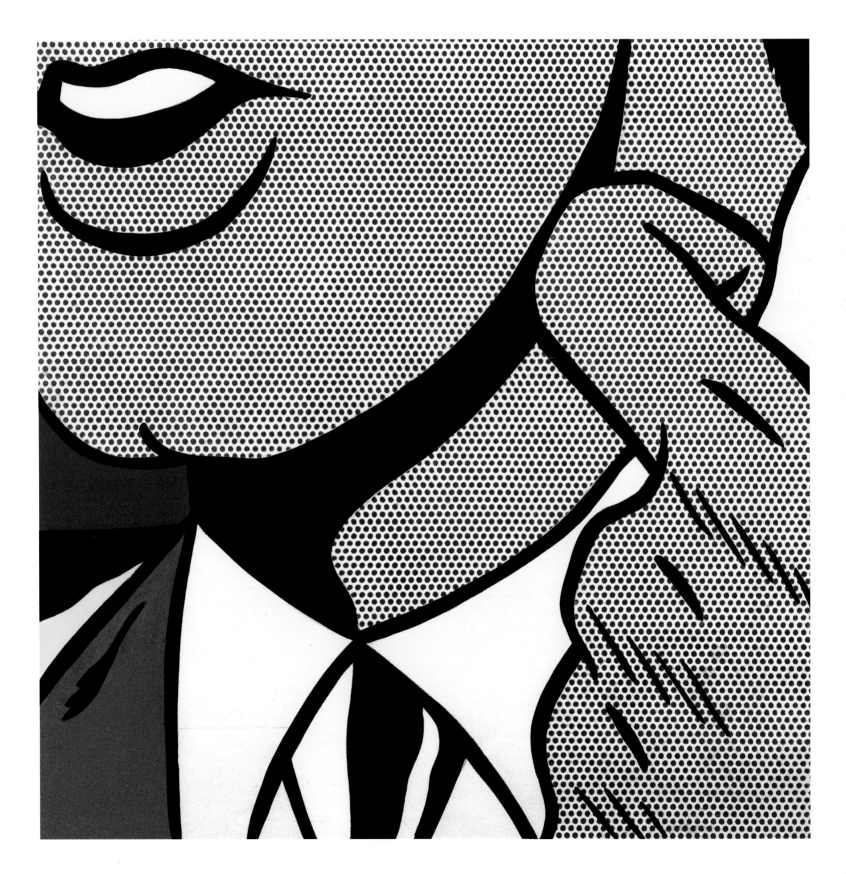

19.
Whaam! 1963
Tate, London

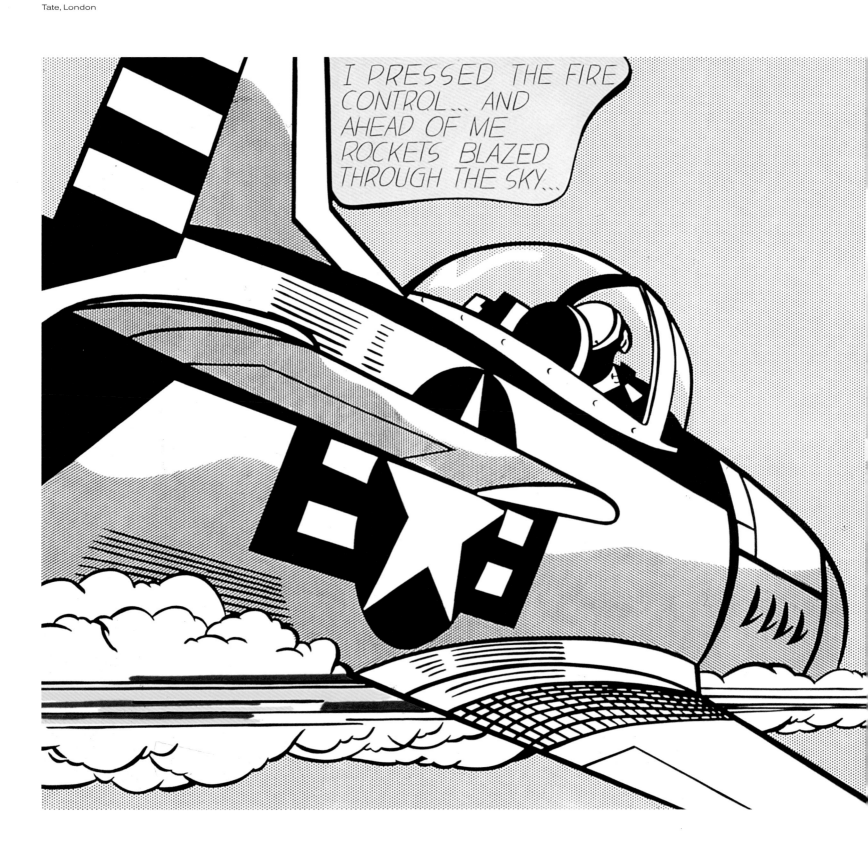

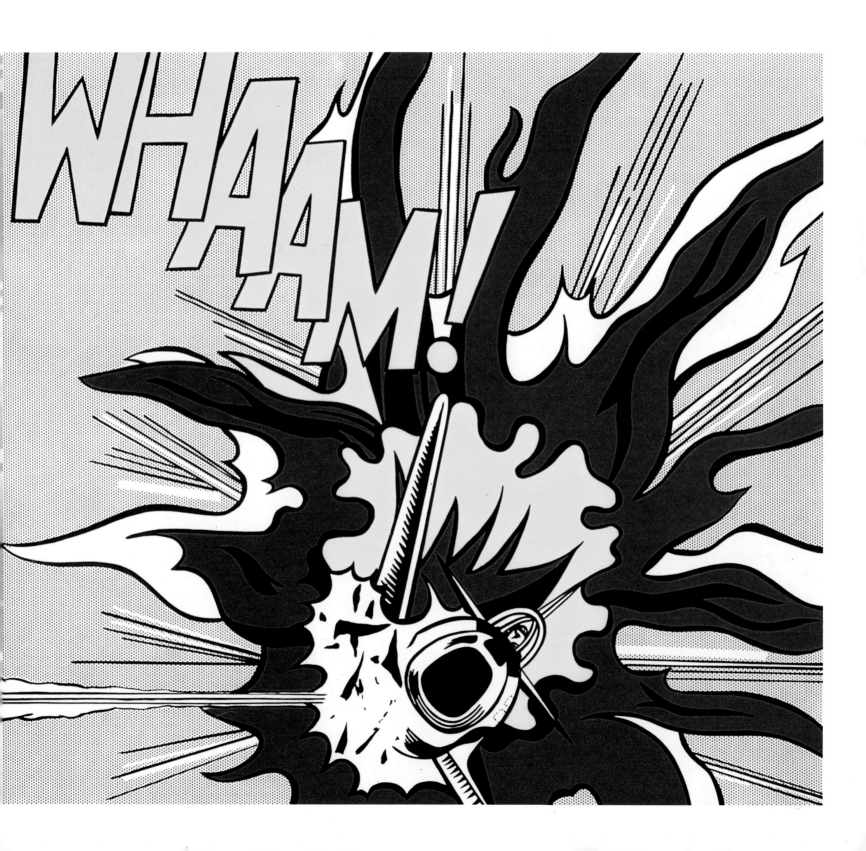

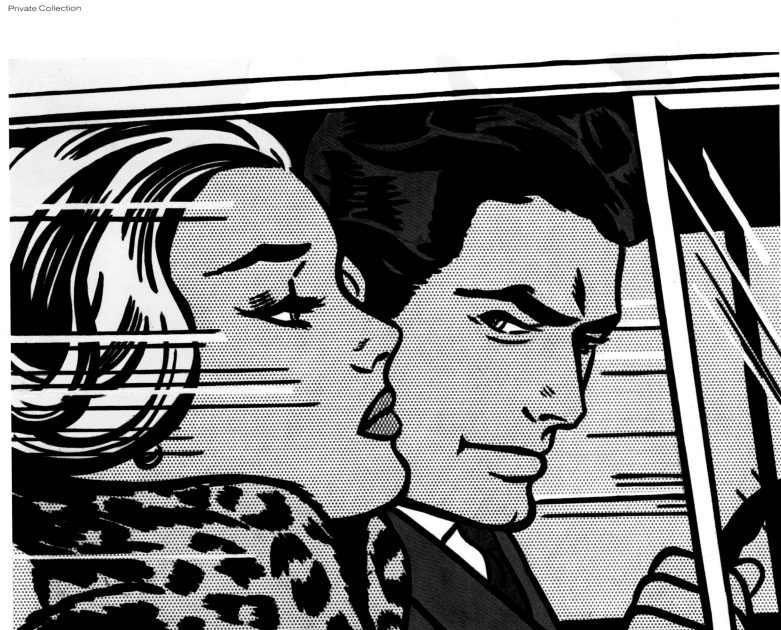

18.
Large Spool. 1963
Sonnabend Collection

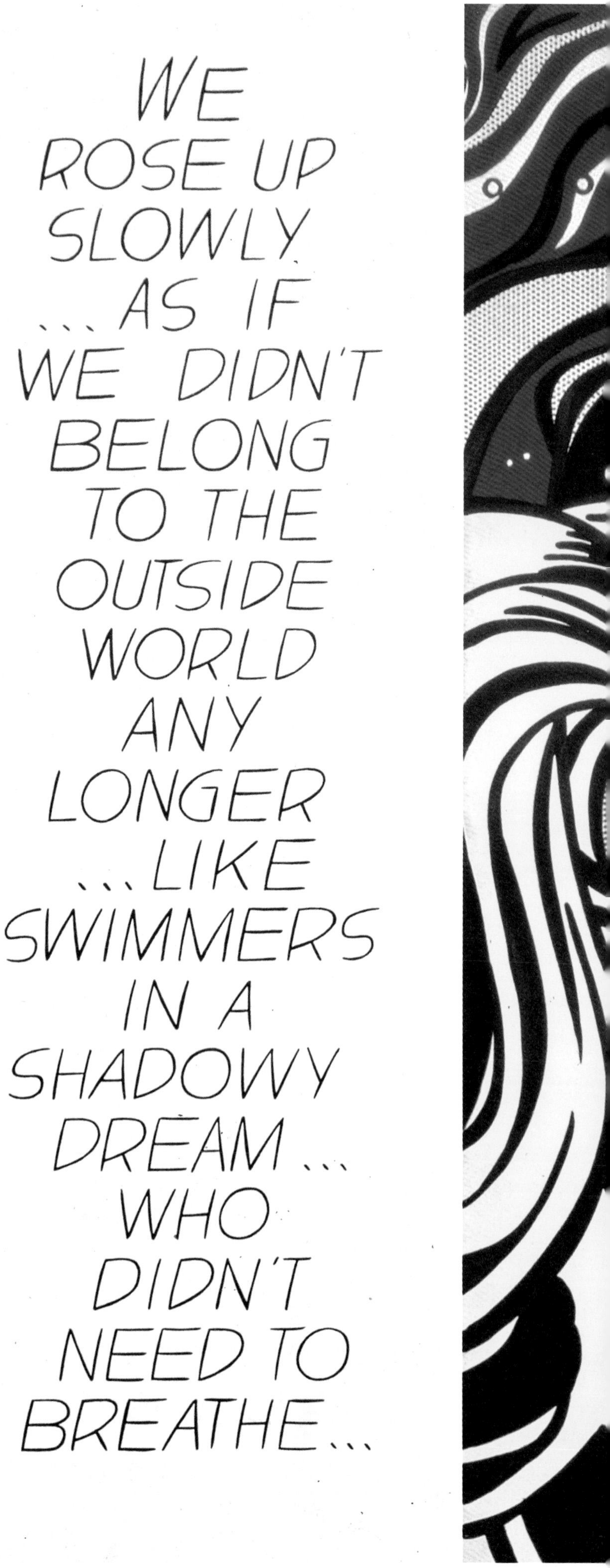

WE
ROSE UP
SLOWLY
... AS IF
WE DIDN'T
BELONG
TO THE
OUTSIDE
WORLD
ANY
LONGER
... LIKE
SWIMMERS
IN A
SHADOWY
DREAM ...
WHO
DIDN'T
NEED TO
BREATHE...

22.
We Rose Up Slowly. 1964
Museum für Moderne Kunst, Frankfurt am Main

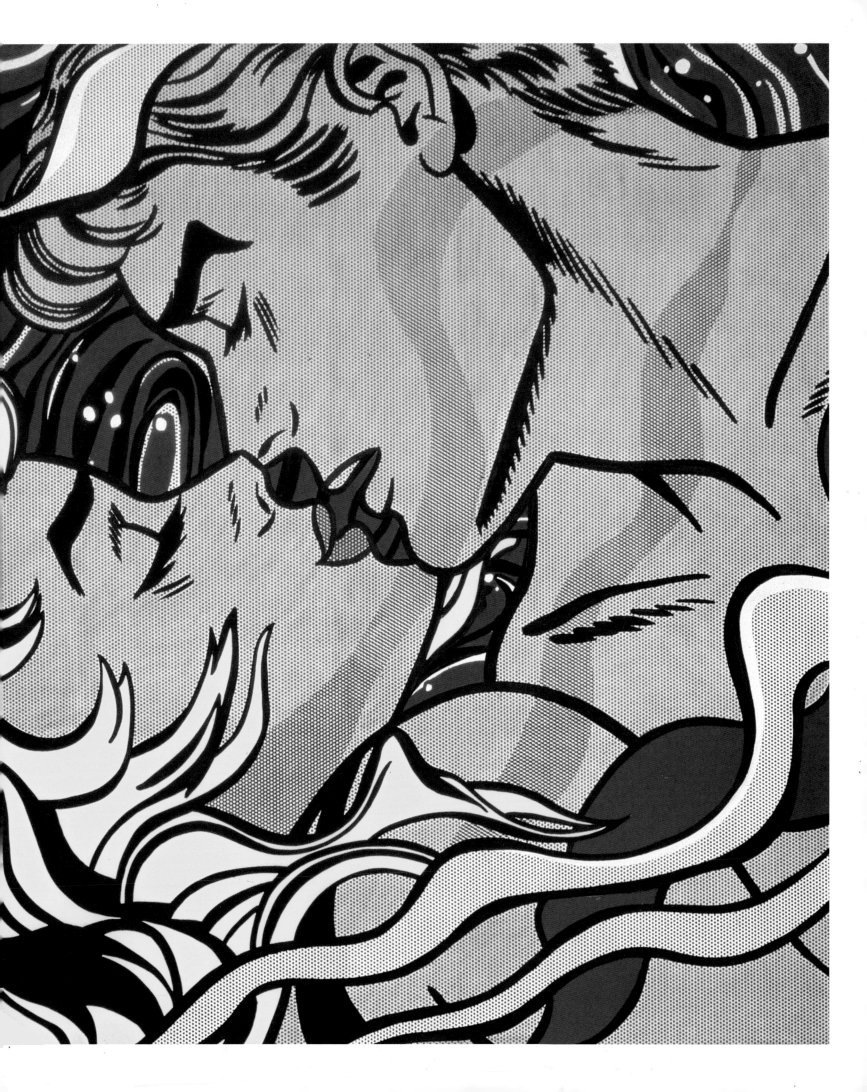

20a.
Ohhh... Alright... 1964
Collection Steve Martin

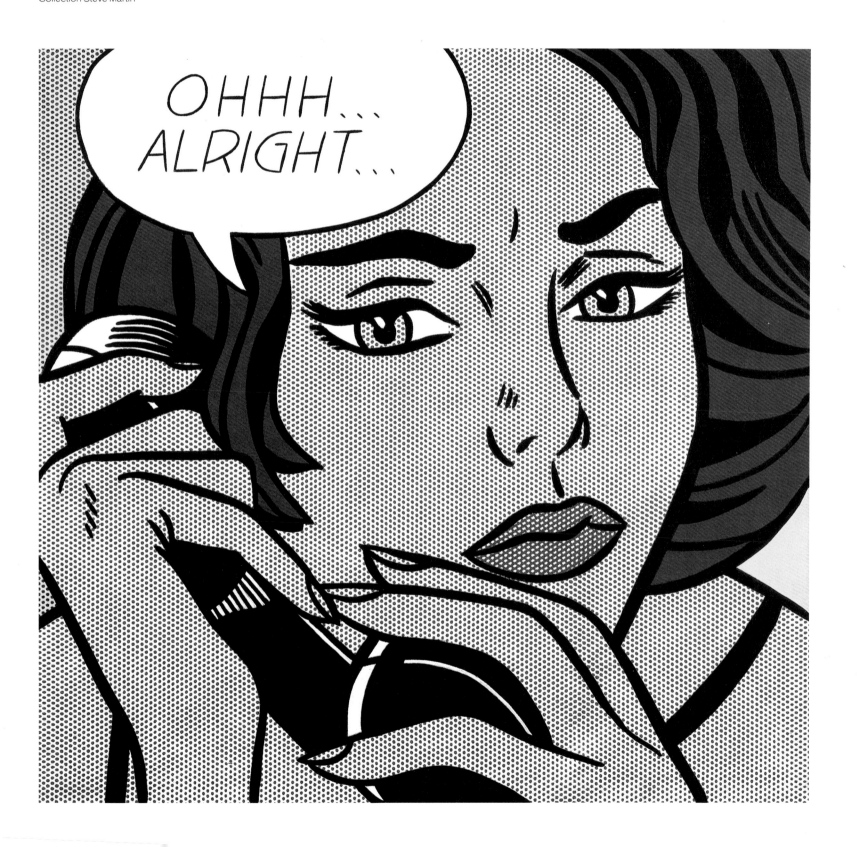

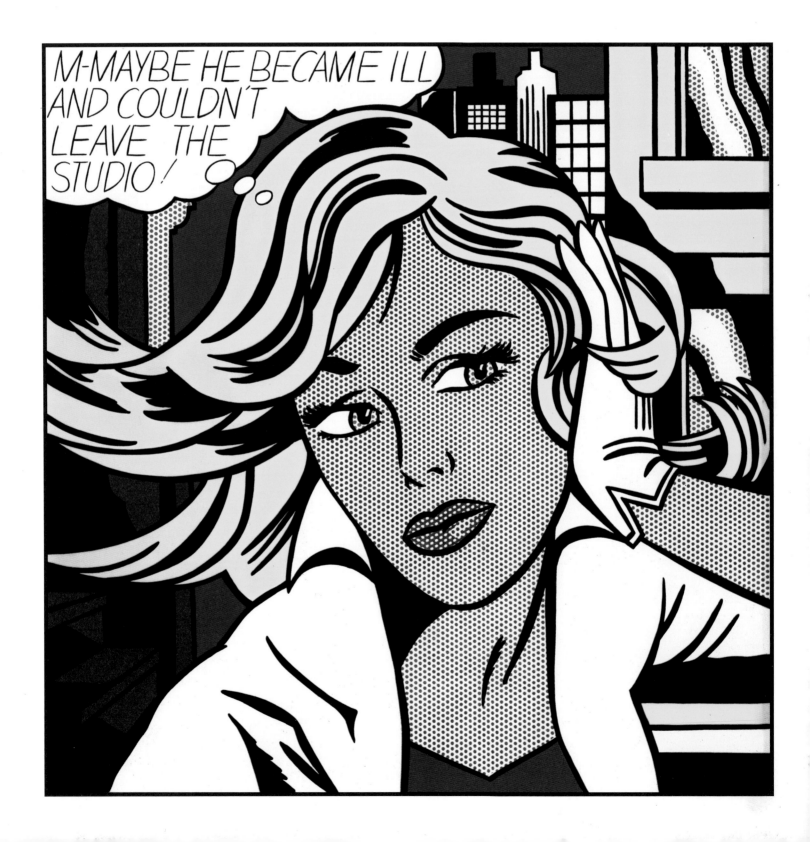

65.
Von Karp. 1963
Private Collection

71.
Drawing for "Grrrrrrrr!". (1965)
Private Collection

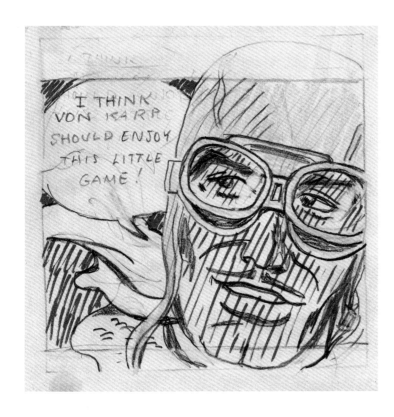

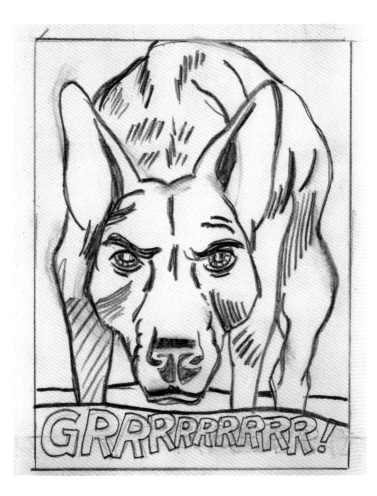

67.
Drawing for "Nurse". 1964
Private Collection

66.
Drawing for "Girl in Mirror". (1964)
Private Collection

82.
Drawing for "Nudes in Mirror". 1994
Private Collection

84.
Sketch, Nude on Phone with Bust. 1995
Private Collection

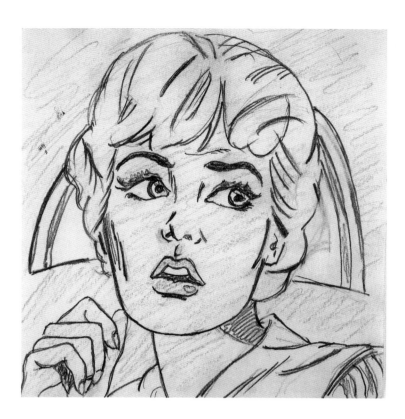

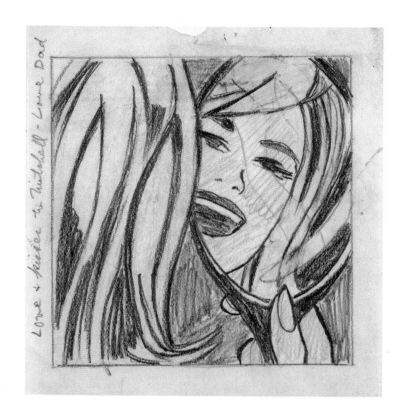

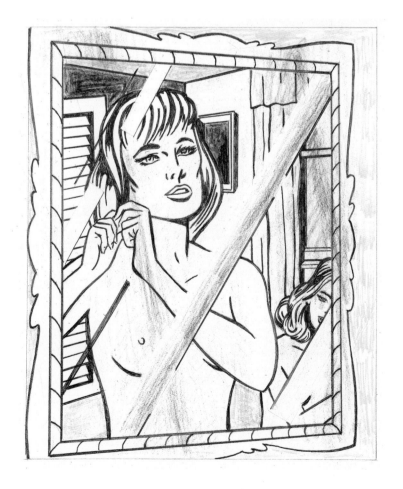

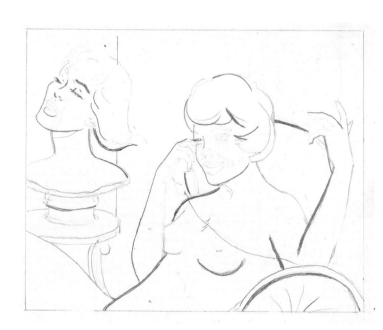

59.
Airplane. 1961
Sonnabend Collection

64.
Man with Coat. 1961
Sonnabend Collection

61.
Girl with Accordion. 1961
Sonnabend Collection

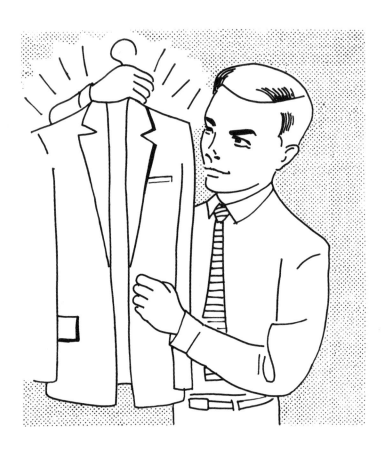

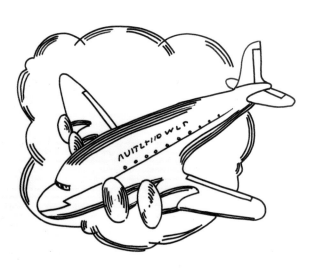

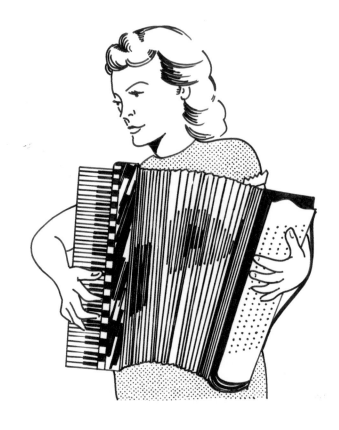

63.
Mail Order Foot. 1961
Sonnabend Collection

60.
Couch. 1961
Sonnabend Collection

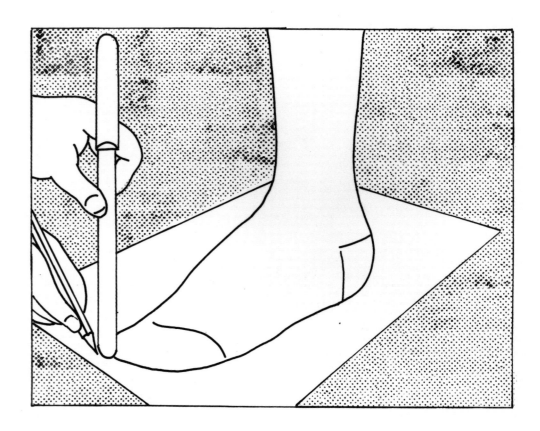

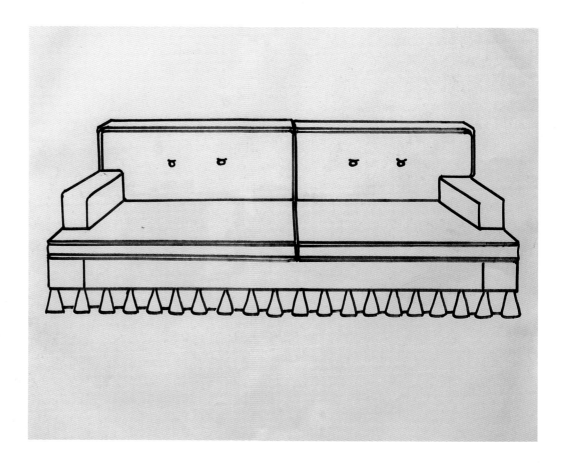

David Sylvester interviews Roy Lichtenstein

New York City, April 1997

David Sylvester: There are times, like the second half of the eighteenth century, when a lot of the best art of a period has humour or wit or irony as an ingredient, and I think that in the last thirty-five years most of the outstanding art has had an element of humour or wit or irony

Roy Lichtenstein: Certainly Miró, Picasso, Klee.

DS: But since then even more, in American art from the beginning of the sixties, in Warhol and Oldenburg and Koons and in Johns too and Rauschenberg and many others, and you've been very much at the centre of all that. Have you produced any art which seems to you *not* to have an element of humour or wit or irony?

RL: Well I'm trying to think. Even the *Entablatures* are meant to be humorous in a way, because they don't seem to be funny but they mean imperial power or something like that. That's the work I can think of that's maybe the most humourless, but it's still meant to be humorous in some way. It's hard to talk about humour without making it very unfunny, but yes. I think that either the subject matter is kind of ridiculous for a painting – you know, a piece of apple pie or something – or the method, the cartooning, kind of says this isn't really a painting, this is really just reproduced trash or something, so that the dots, black lines, things like that, sort of tell you that is not serious art. I think that, say, Picasso's rendering of Delacroix or Velázquez could probably look like a sort of trashy copy of a masterpiece. So I think that some of the humour started there.

DS: Did you think when you started to do these parodies that you were doing something that Picasso had done? Did that sort of give you licence? Or did you only realise afterwards?

RL: I realised afterwards. Picasso's always been such a huge influence that I thought when I started the cartoon paintings that I was getting away from Picasso, and even my cartoons of Picasso were done almost to rid myself of his influence. I don't think that I'm over his influence but they probably don't look like Picassos; Picasso himself would probably have thrown up looking at my pictures.

DS: If I remember the dates, if I'm not getting confused, during the early period of Pop Art at the very beginning of the sixties you were already doing Picasso parodies, weren't you? You were starting almost at the time of the Popeyes?

RL: Yes, same year.

DS: You've done parodies of a whole range of modern styles. Have you had in your mind a number of things which had suggested themselves and were lining up waiting to be done, or did you come upon your models in the course of time?

RL: I think I just came upon them. I had no programme; I always thought each one was the last. But then I'd see something like a way of doing a Monet through just dots that would look like a machine-made Impressionist painting. But then it took me a long time even to do Léger, which seemed like the obvious person for me to do. I'd probably done a little bit of Léger in the context I think of those *trompe l'oeil* paintings, where there were little pieces of Léger tacked on the wall. Yes, each thing was separate.

DS: Have you had series which you started and which you quickly realised were duds?

RL: You know I get ideas like when I'm waking up in the morning or something like that and I kind of sometimes scribble them down and then when I wake up I realise that there's absolutely no way to create a visual counterpart of what I thought of that makes any sense. They usually don't get to be paintings. I give up on an idea if there's no way to make it into something that says something I haven't said or if there's just no visual correlate to it. Sometimes I find this later. That happened a bit with the *Mirrors*. I get the idea of doing mirrors, and they didn't look like mirrors and they didn't look very interesting, and it just took time to get something that was an interesting enough abstraction and that people could take for a mirror – you kind of learn a mirror the same way you learn a thing is a brush-stroke. I had trouble with the Brush-strokes too: they looked like slices of bacon or something, they didn't really look anything like brush-strokes when I started. And I got this idea that I would use India ink on acetate and make a brush-stroke, and it made a very interesting brush-stroke, because the acetate kind of repels the ink. And then I would copy, I would draw pictures of those and it was just a way of getting an idea for a brush-stroke. It had more interest than I could get by trying to dream one up.

DS: So you had a lot of difficulty in realising one of your most preposterous ideas, an idea that subverted a whole mystique of painting?

RL: Yes, it was interesting to do, in a meticulous or maybe classical way, a bravura gesture which had a completely different meaning – the idea that you make a mark on the canvas and you see what that suggests and you make another mark and you try to form a unity of positions and tone and so forth just interacting with what you have.

DS: But maybe that was the mystique rather than the reality?

RL: Yes, it could be, because people say Franz Kline actually projected pictures of his brush-strokes on the canvas and kind of made brush-strokes almost in the same way that I did. Of course, he wasn't drawing a picture of a brush-stroke exactly, but he had an idea of the composition before he started. I suppose to think that you just do some mindless thing probably never was the case. But certainly the Abstract Expressionists were in a more romantic mode of painting, or give and take, than my paintings are seen to be anyway. Because I want them to look as though I never corrected anything and it just came out that way. But I go through all sorts of contortions to make it look that way. Because I want them to look kind of like a commercial product but at the same time I want them to be an interesting painting, and so between drawings and collages and all sorts of things that lead up to the painting there's a lot of changes that go on.

DS: All the paintings you do obviously begin with a work on paper?

RL: Practically all of them, unless they're so simple that they can just be conceived of.

DS: If there are going to be departures from the original sketch, at what stage do they tend to occur?

RL: Well, recently I've been doing collages between the drawing and the painting.

DS: When you say recently ...

RL: Well I would say the *Interiors*, from there forward.

DS: The new Interiors or the early nineties *Interiors*?

RL: The early nineties *Interiors*. And often with more complex paintings before that. But when I worked on a painting I would do it from a drawing but I would put certain things I was fairly sure I wanted in the painting, and then collage on the painting with printed dots or painted paper or something before I really committed it. And then it's not impossible at all to change the painting.

The colour I use is soluble and I can take off whole areas of paint and put them in again, so it's not impossible to make changes which don't show.

DS: Did you come upon the idea of using collage that way entirely on your own, or were you inspired by the way in which Mondrian used tape?

RL: Well I seem to have always known that Mondrian used tape, but I think I had a teacher who used collage a little even though they were sort of expressionist paintings. He would try out colour just by taking a piece of coloured paper and putting it there to see whether that was the direction he wanted to go in.

DS: Who was that?

RL: Hoyt Sherman. He was my mentor at Ohio State, and I probably got it from him.

DS: And how precisely have you been using it in the recent interiors?

RL: Well, the collages are very similar to the paintings. But in fact a lot of work was done there. I try to strengthen and redraw and do all sorts of things to the painting, so it isn't just a copy of the collage. But many of them look like copies of the collages, I must say. Although probably everything is in a slightly different place, and there's some other colour changes and things like that, the painting is still very much like the collage. I try to draw it over again, you know, by drawing upside down and doing everything I can to suppress the subject matter, so I can make the painting work.

DS: You use a ratio of one to four between the collage and the painting in the new group?

RL: Yes.

DS: And what about the big Interiors of the early nineties?

RL: I don't think we had any particular formula. I think I would do a collage and might … In fact we did project the slide on the wall and see how big do I really want to make this painting, and do something like that, just to get a feel of how big they were going to be. Of course, we wanted those *Interiors* to be large, so they would make you feel as though you could walk into them, but they're so stylised that you obviously don't think it's reality, but when you make it about life size, something peculiar happens when you stand in front of an interior.

DS: Can you go into more detail about precisely how you use the collage?

RL: Well, I have some idea in the little sketch that I make, and I start out that way, and I have these printed dots of all kinds of gradations and sizes and colours and painted paper with just all the colours I usually use. And I start with a sketch in mind and try to do something like that. But as it develops I can see that it could use something more daring in the colour over here, or this could be pushed a little bit up there, and maybe the sizes of the areas aren't right. So I can easily make changes. When they were done with black lines, which these aren't, except the few with black lines in them, I would start with photographer's tape and just draw them with strands of it and make a drawing. And the problem with colouring in a black and white drawing is that it's very hard to get the colour to work, because you've already made the drawing static – you know the sizes can't change very well – but the reason I use tape is because it makes a very decisive line. But it's immediately changeable, you can cut off a little bit, take it off and put it on again. That's like Mondrian, a little bit. I think that you can make the line you want to end up with, which gives you the black of the line, and it's definite, but it's very moveable, and I like that a lot. It looks etched in stone, but it isn't. I like to be able to manipulate all of this, but I like it to look as though it was never changed, that that's just the way it was, that you guessed right the first time. That's part of the style of it, I guess.

DS: You're what's called a classical artist.

RL: When I'm not called something else. Yes, you know sometimes, we started out thinking out how strange our painting was next to normal painting, which was anything expressionist. You forget that this has been thirty-five years now and people don't look at it as if it were same kind of oddity.

DS: Well, I'm happy to say that in 1963 I said you were the heir to Chardin and Poussin. French Classicism.

RL: Both of them seem static, set in stone, the same sort of thing that I'm trying to do in my style. And artificial. It's probably true. I wish it were true.

DS: I think it is true.

RL: I think that one of the changes I made in the recent *Interiors* is that the lines aren't all black and I use different colour lines, but, say, if I use yellow lines on the chair, I'll use it on part of the chair and part of the wall and part of the floor, or whatever, so it makes a little locality of yellow, but doesn't surround any particular object pattern, it doesn't surround the whole chair, for instance. The other part of the chair might be grey or black or something else, and that would go off somewhere. I use it so that the colours of the lines make areas in the same way that the tone, the gradated dots, say, go through a number of objects. I mean, once in a while, they're on a single object, but they can go through a whole group.

It's a little bit the way *chiaroscuro* isn't just shadows but a way of combining the figure and the background, or whatever's near it in a dark area. It really didn't have to fill in the entire object pattern the way, say, Byzantine painting would do, where the colour of the face was a face-colour and the colour of the robe was something else, red or something, and it had to permeate the whole object. And so I think of *chiaroscuro* as a way of only maybe half the figure's dark, and the other half's light. You're not confined to the object pattern, but the subject matter excuse for this is that it's a shadow. And that's interesting to me,

But anyway, I've been using gradated dots or colours that go from one form to another, but the idea is that the lines could get like that to make areas or localities of the things that are independent. Of course, they don 't look like anything in nature, so there's no subject matter excuse – though we don't really have to use excuses, I think, after Mondrian or Picasso or Cézanne. So it's just an idea that occurred to me, not because I thought out all of that logic, but because it just occurred to me that I could just do this side of the chair in orange, and that side in blue – however I wanted to do it. So, that's that idea. And I think that at least differentiates these from any other paintings; I don't think I've ever done anything like this before.

And then some of the lines are little sort of notes. You know, in the middle of, say, this area of red lines let's say there might be one black line that stands out and has nothing to do with the subject matter either, but just they're little points of colour that I've spotted around. And it has the effect of making it sort of figure and the surrounding area ground, but the surrounding area might be several objects. It's somewhat the way *chiaroscuro* is used: a little point of light in the middle of a dark area or dark in the middle of a light area. So I'm trying to do something like that, putting colour with subject matter. If you did it without the subject matter you wouldn't know this was being done, so the subject matter helps because there's a reference to reality. Some kind of reality, anyway.

David Sylvester, who died in 2001, was an internationally renowned art critic and a regular contributor to the art pages of *The London Review of Books*. In 1993 he became the first art critic to receive a Golden Lion at the Venice Biennale. His works include a number of books on art and interviews with artists including the universally acclaimed *On Modern Art* (Chatto and Windus, London 1996), *Looking at Giacometti* (Chatto and Windus, London 1994) and *Interviews with Francis Bacon* (ed.), (Thames and Hudson, London 1975).

The above interview with Roy Lichtenstein is reprinted by kind permission from the David Sylvester Literary Trust represented by Clintons Solicitors, London, and from Anthony D'Offay, the original publisher of this interview in *Some Kind of Reality* (London 1997).

8.
ART. 1962
Gordon Locksley and
Dr. George T. Shea Collection, USA

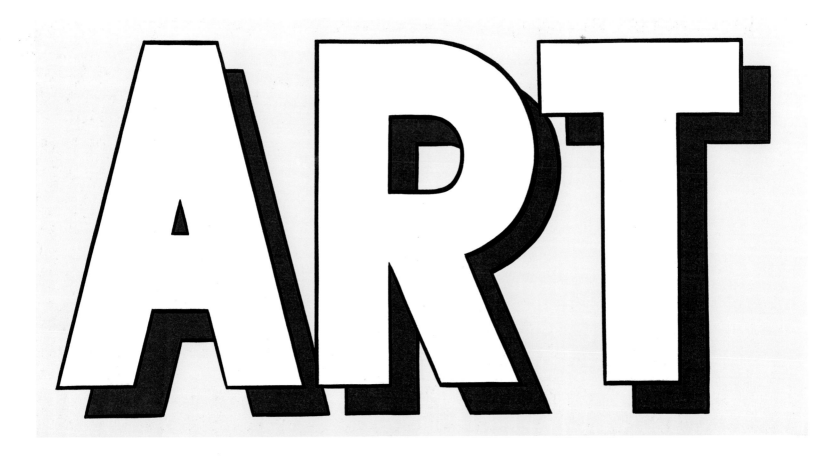

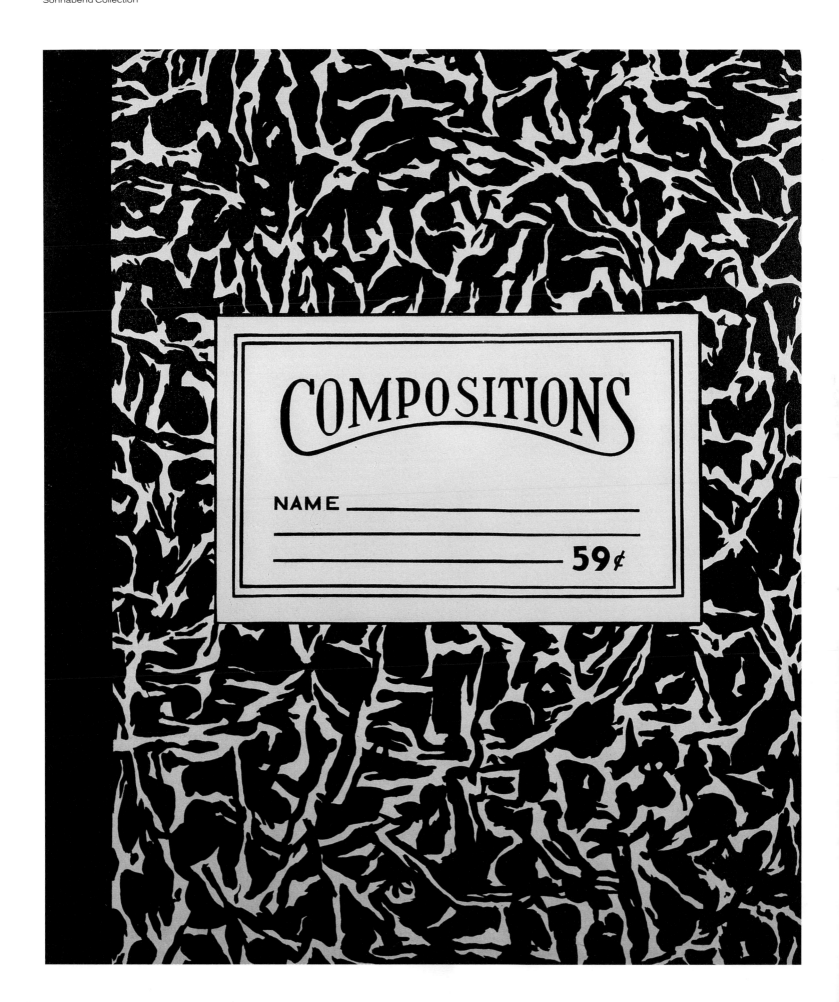

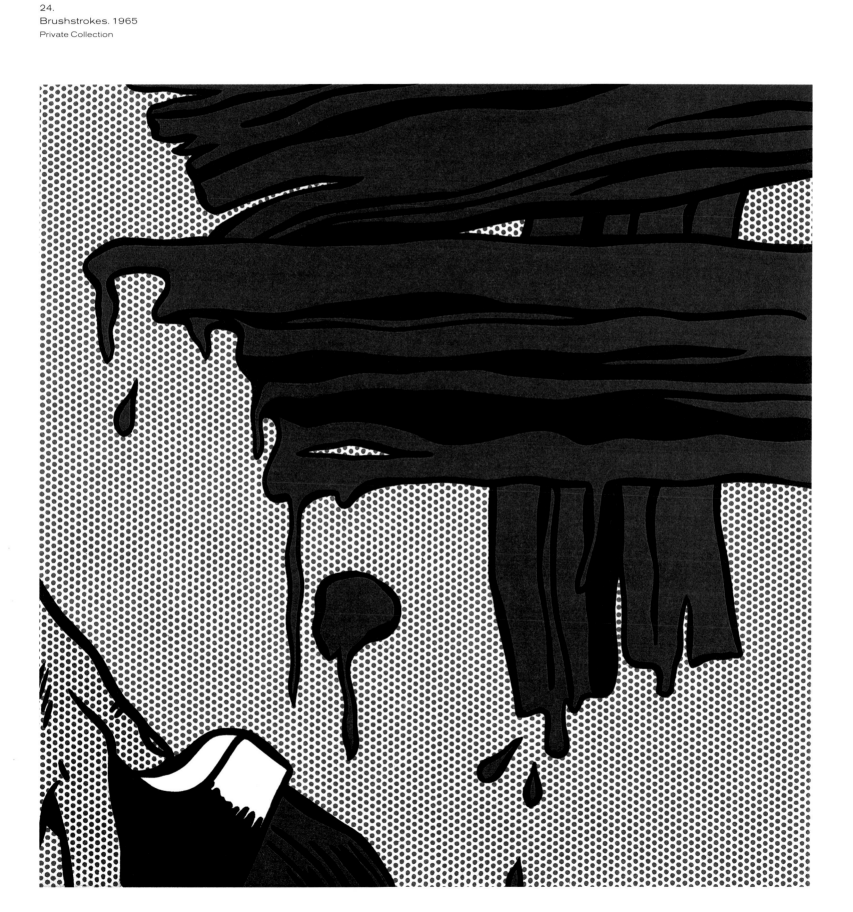

16.
Image Duplicator. 1963
Collection Charles Simonyi, Seattle

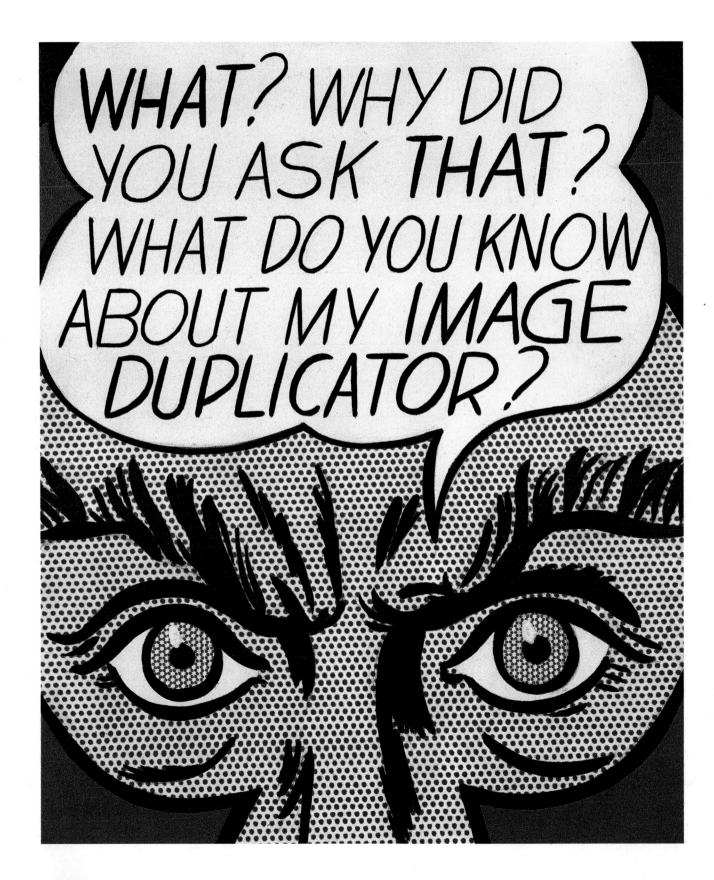

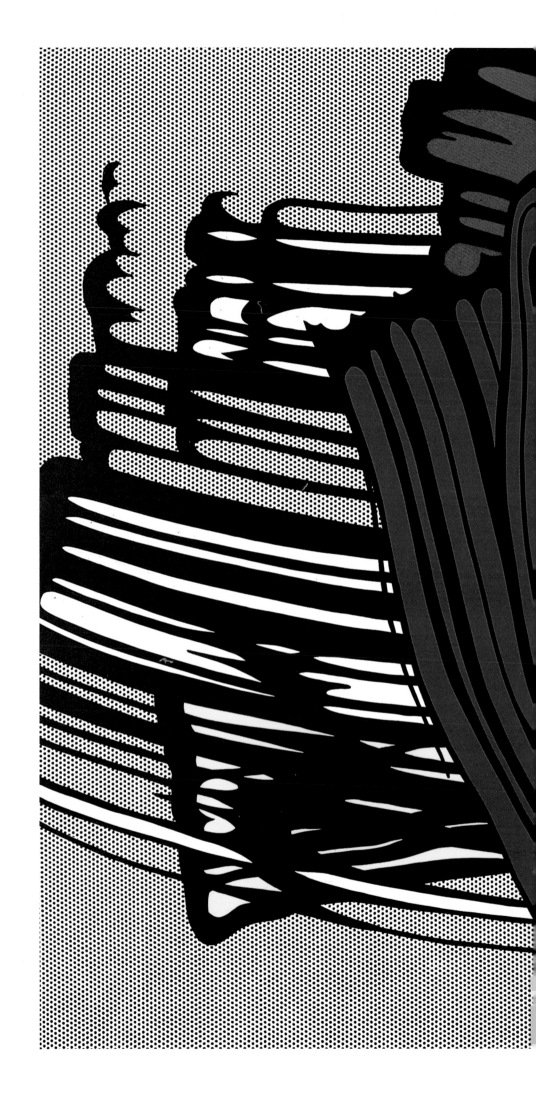

23.
Big Painting VI. 1965
Kunstsammlung Nordrhein-Westfalen,
Düsseldorf

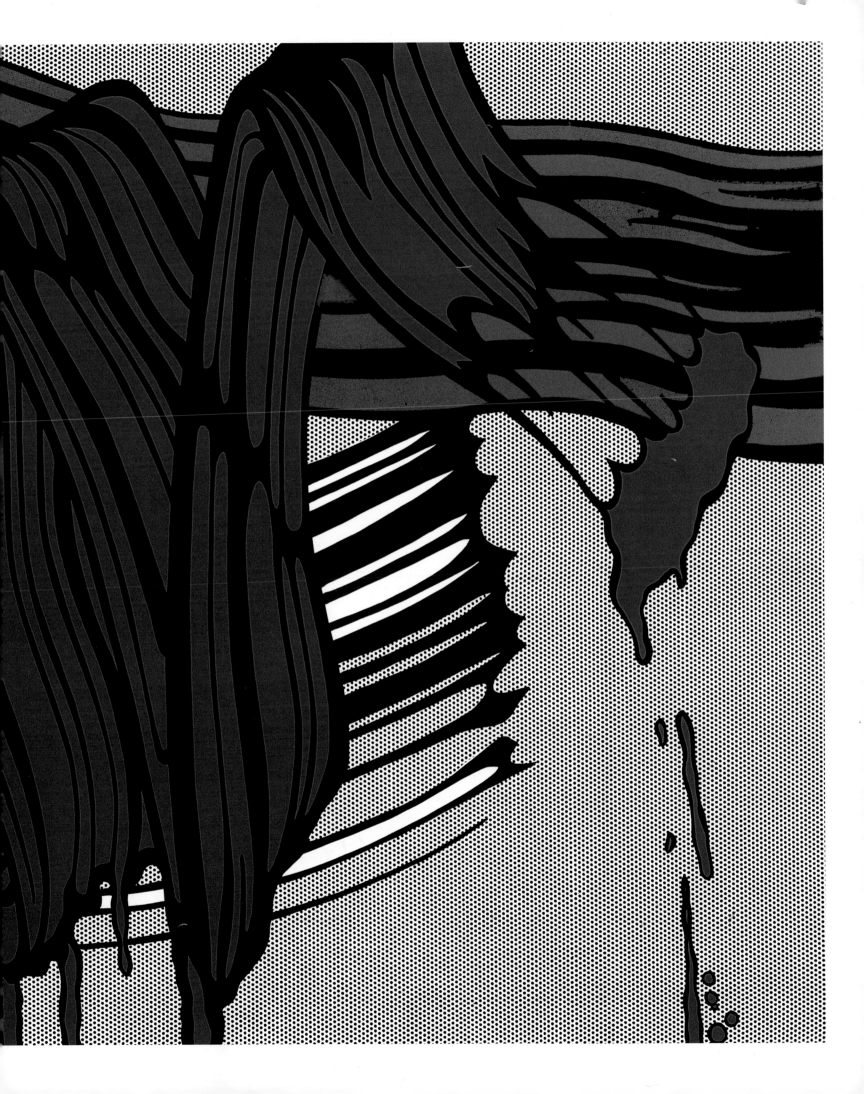

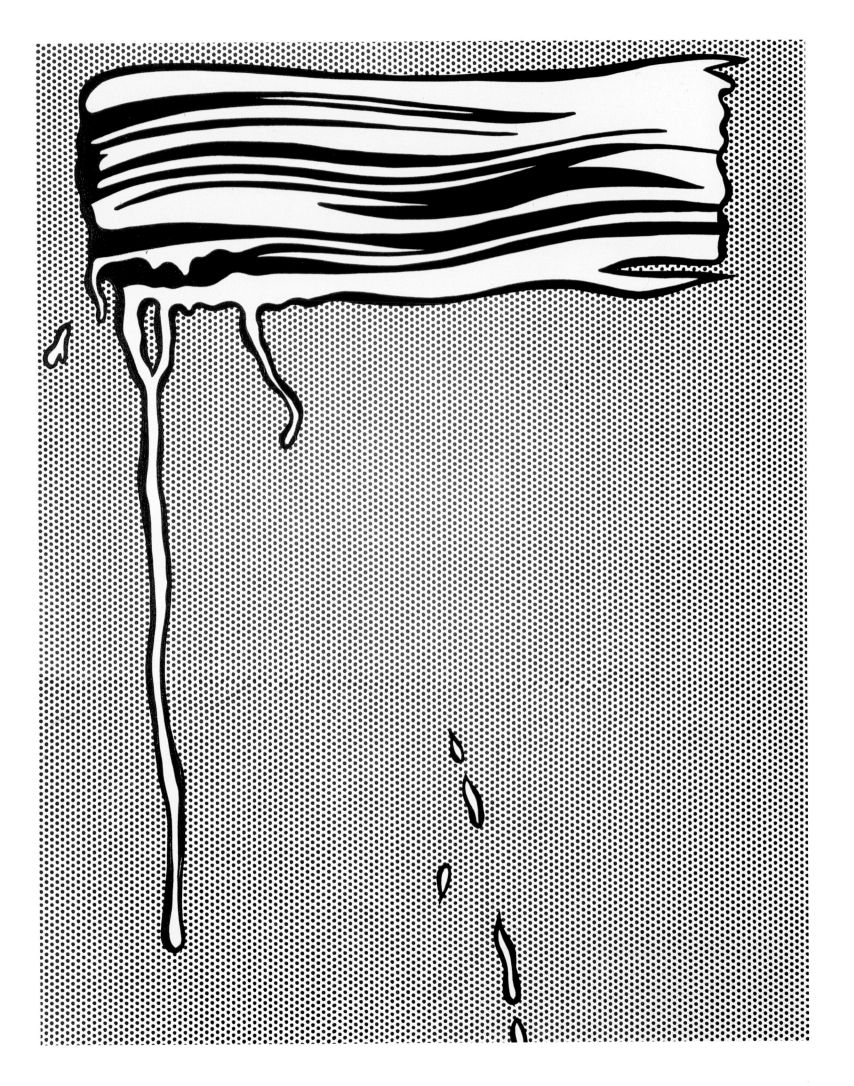

27.
Yellow Brushstroke I. 1965
Kunsthaus Zürich

29.
Stretcher Frame with Cross Bars III. 1968
Private Collection

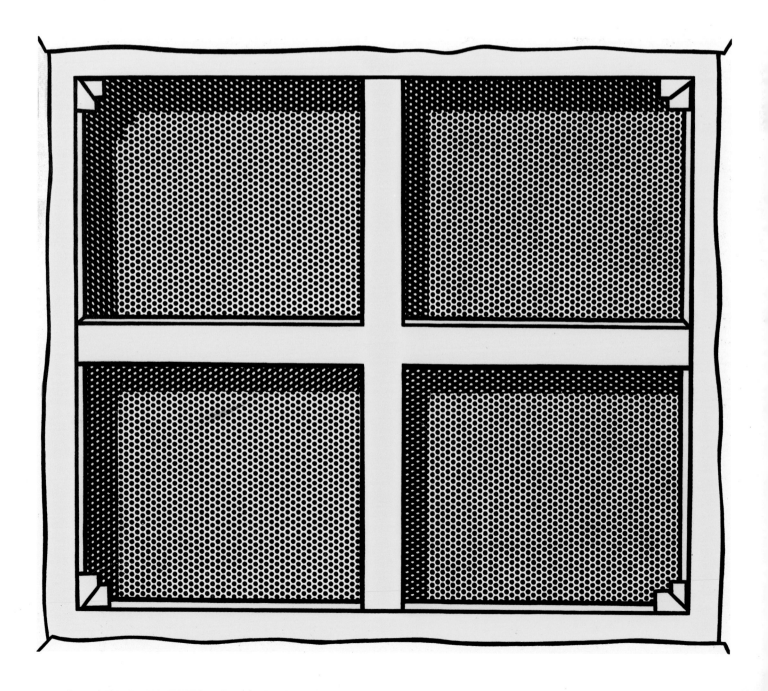

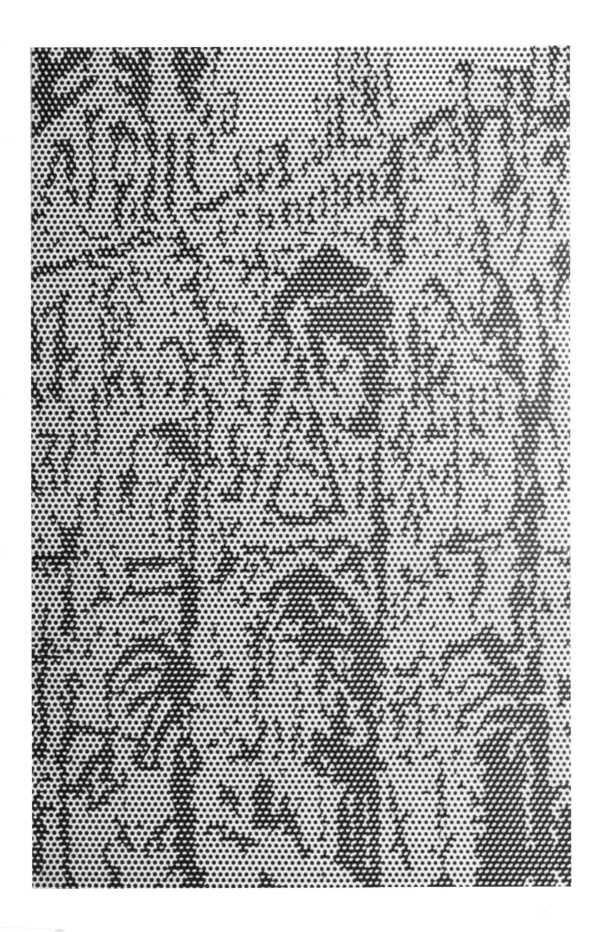

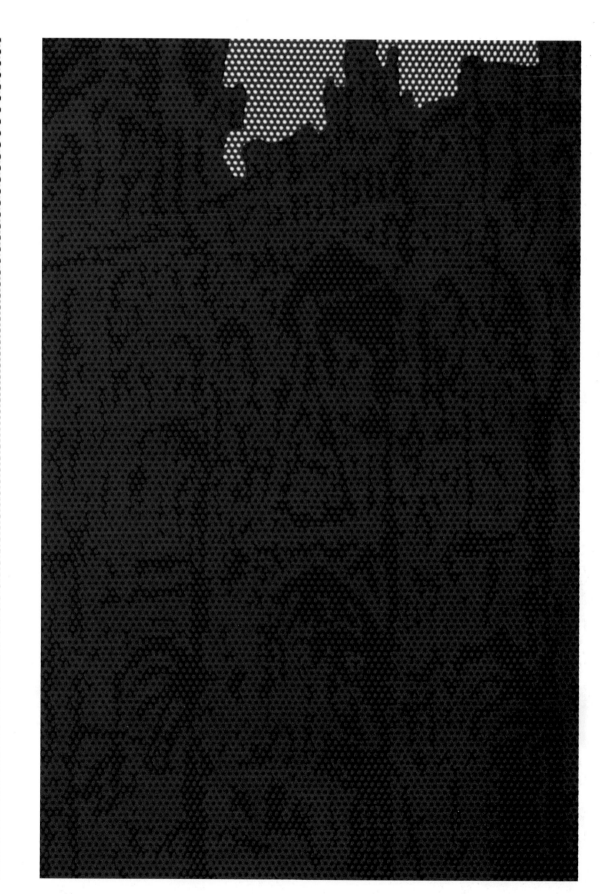

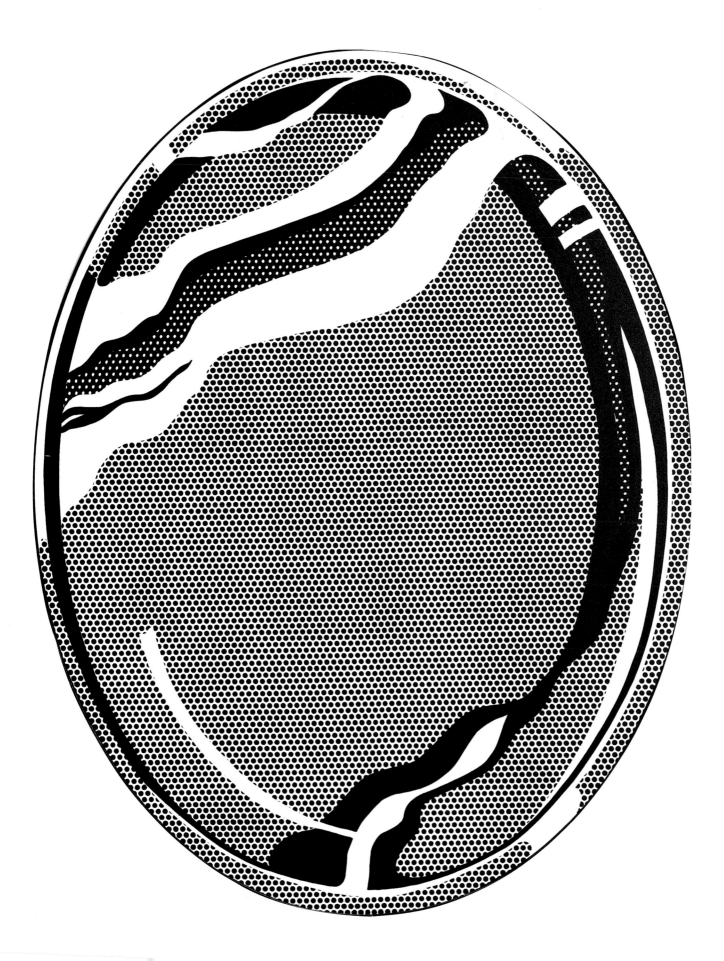

30.
Mirror #1. 1969
The Eli and Edythe L. Broad Collection

32.
Mirror in Six Panels. 1971
Roy Lichtenstein Foundation Collection

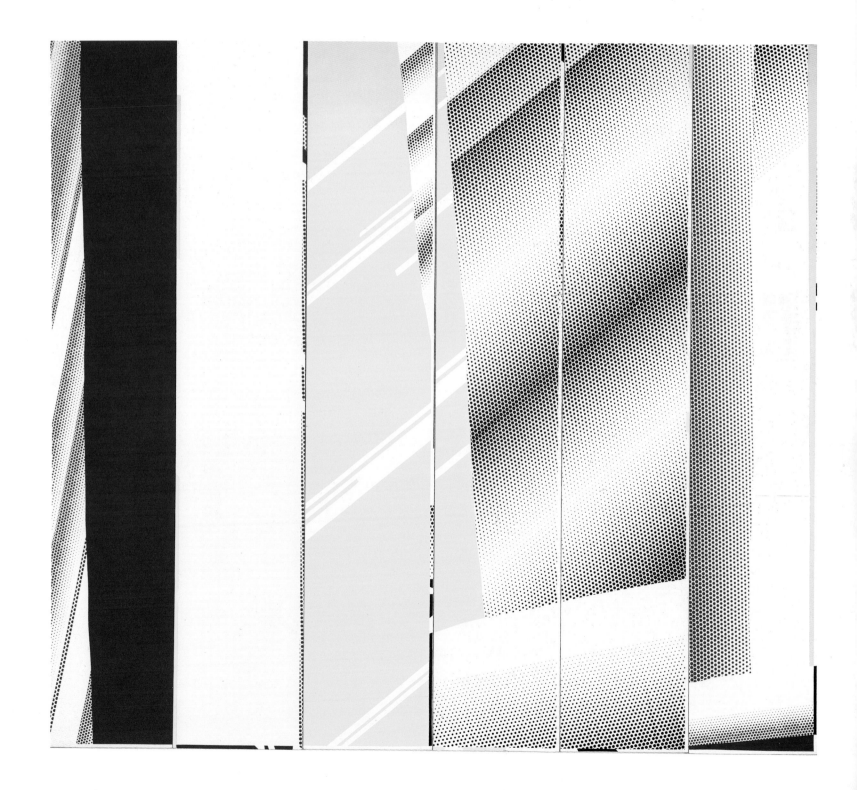

38.
Entablature. 1974
Private Collection

39.
Entablature. 1974
Private Collection

37.
Stretcher Frame Revealed
Beneath Painting of a Stretcher Frame. 1973
Private Collection

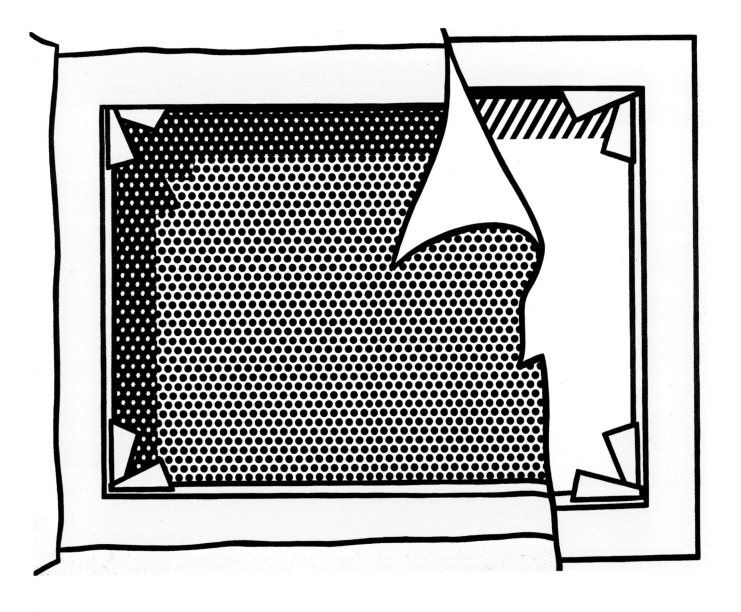

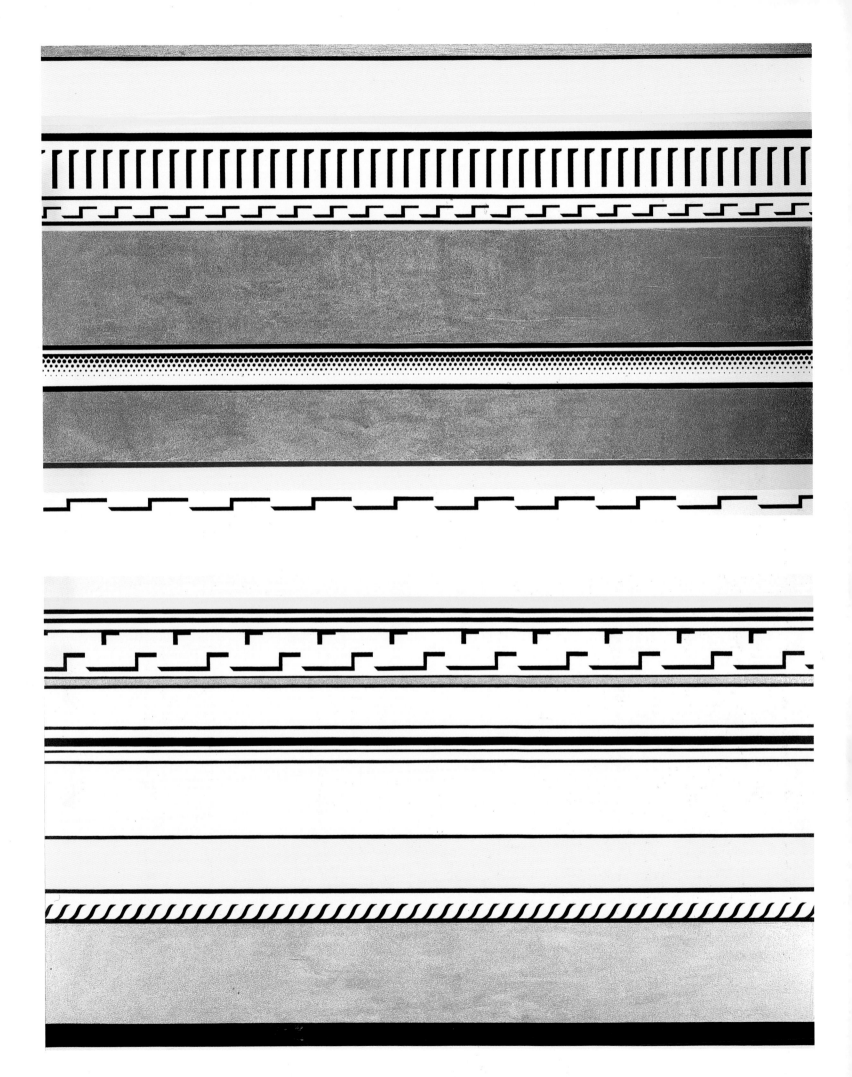

44.
Self Portrait. 1978
Private Collection

42.
Portrait. 1977
Private Collection

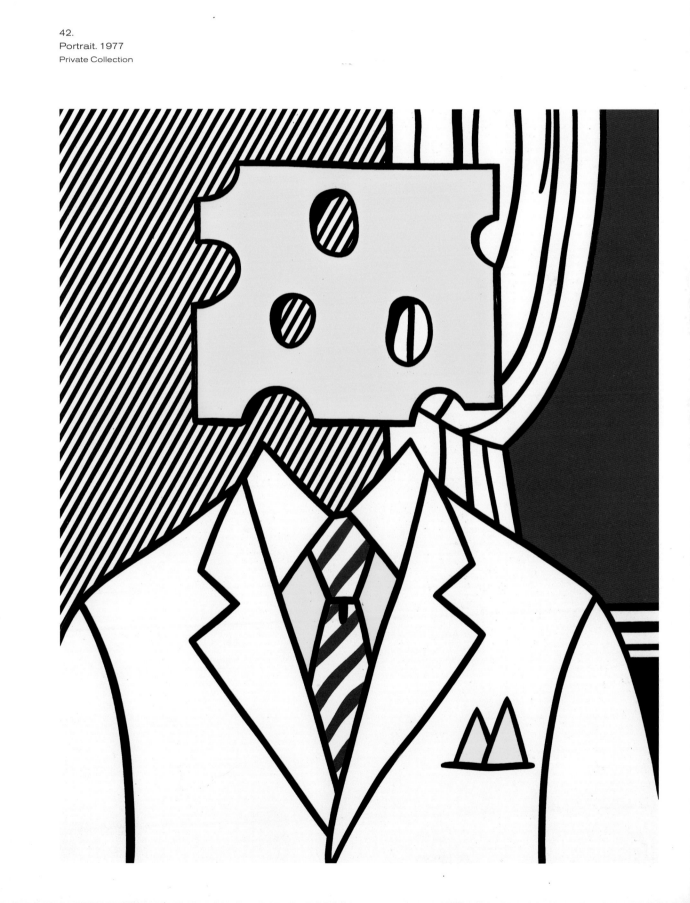

47.
Painting with Scattered Brushstrokes. 1984
Private Collection

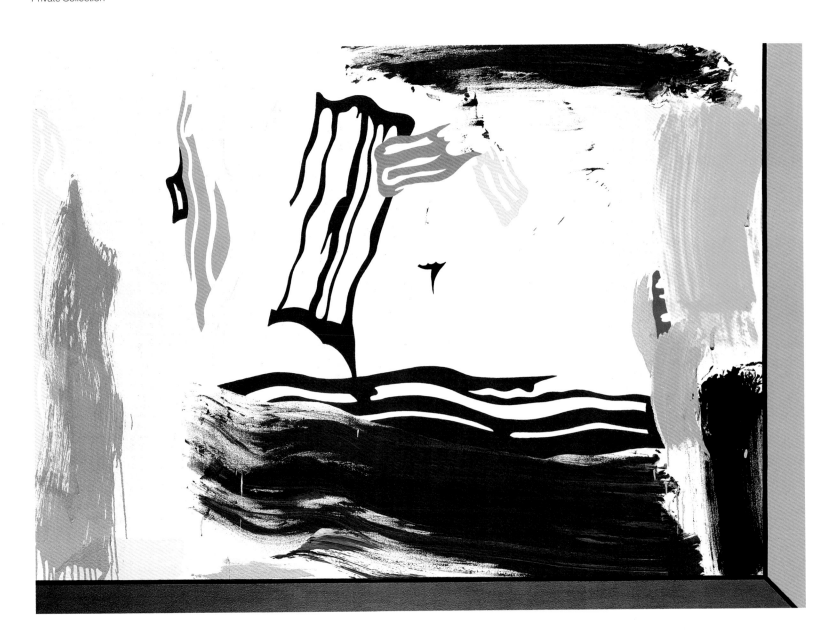

46.
Painting: Bamboo Frame. 1984
Private Collection

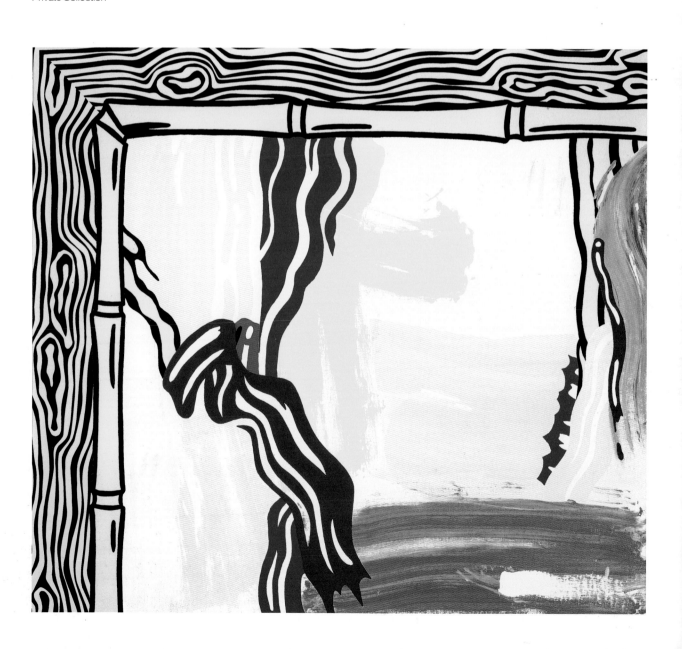

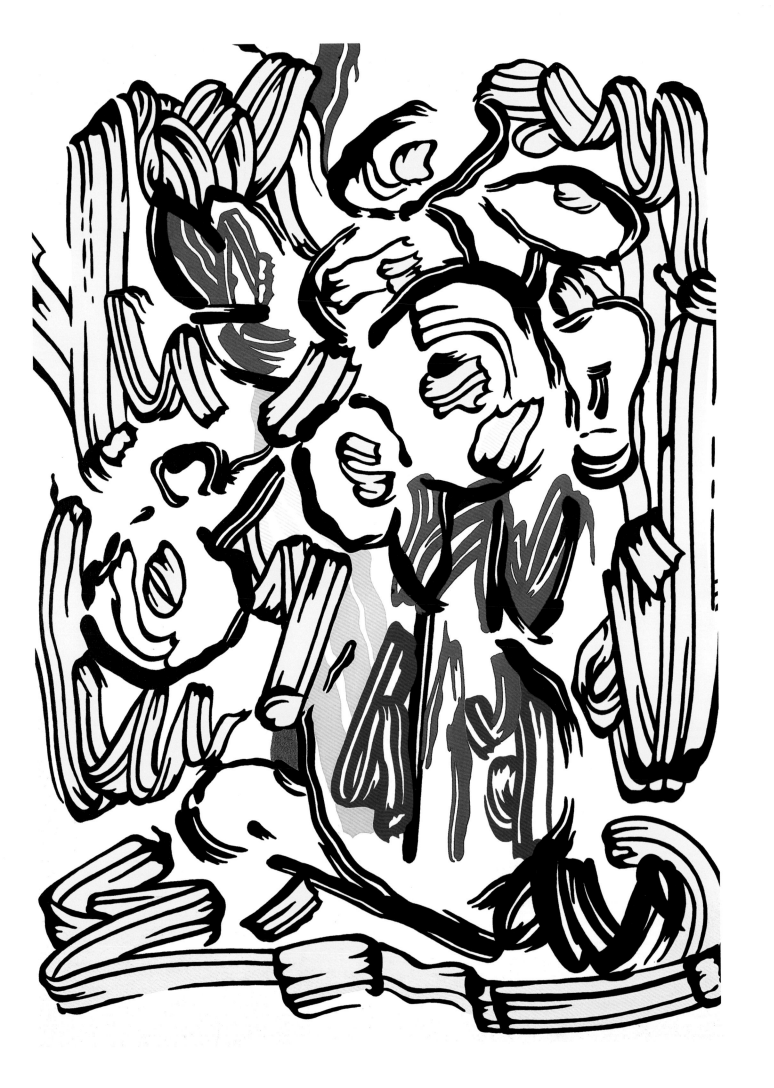

45.
Flowers. 1982
Private Collection

48.
Reflections: Art. 1988
Private Collection

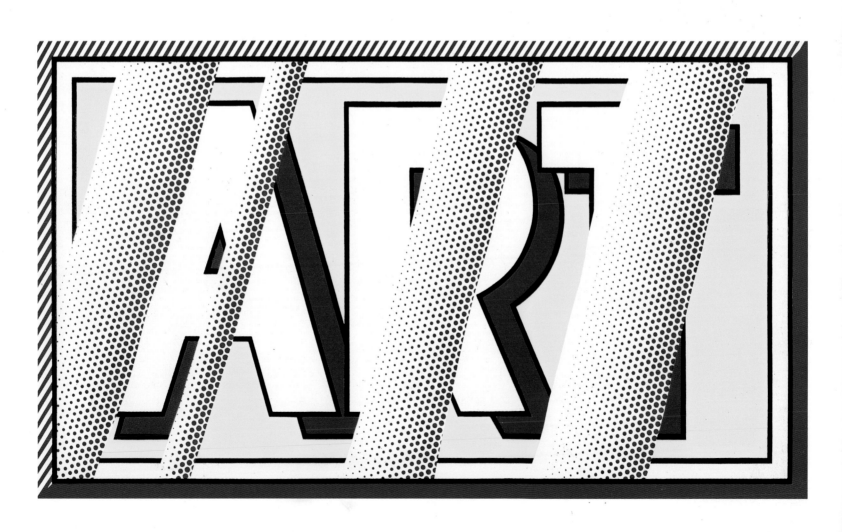

Michael Lobel

Pop Art According to Lichtenstein

In a landmark 1963 interview, Roy Lichtenstein responded to the critic Gene Swenson's question "What is Pop Art?" with the following:

I don't know – the use of commercial art as subject matter in painting, I suppose. It was hard to get a painting that was despicable enough so that no one would hang it – everybody was hanging everything. It was almost acceptable to hang a dripping paint rag, everybody was accustomed to this. The one thing everyone hated was commercial art; apparently they didn't hate that enough either. [1]

For anyone attempting to understand Lichtenstein's role in the emergence of Pop Art in New York in the early 1960s, there is a great deal of meaning to be unpacked in these four short sentences. If the artist offers us a cursory yet workable definition of Pop Art ("the use of commercial art as subject matter in painting") he seems unsure or ambivalent about that definition, as signaled by the equivocating asides – "I don't know" and "I suppose" – that bookend his statement. He goes on to frame Pop as a response to the status of painting at the time. Although he no doubt recognized the achievements of earlier Abstract Expressionist painters like Jackson Pollock and Willem de Kooning, his ironic observation that it "was almost acceptable to hang a dripping paint rag" suggests that he perceived the possibilities of gestural painting to be thoroughly exhausted by that time. Finally, although he concludes by pointing to what was initially considered so threatening about Pop – its embrace of the commercial world that had been so thoroughly rejected by an earlier generation of modernist painters – he quickly adds an ironic rejoinder: "…apparently they didn't hate that enough either." In other words, Pop already seemed to have achieved a too comfortable position of critical and institutional acceptance only two years after its initial appearance on the New York art scene.

The equivocal and ironic tone of Lichtenstein's response suggests that he recognized that the categorization of his work as Pop Art was something of a mixed blessing. The identification of him as a Pop artist certainly provided him a significant amount of attention, both within the art world and from the public at large; it also offered a convenient category through which his work could be marketed to collectors, museums and the public. Yet he may very well have recognized that this act of labeling had the potential to ascribe a fairly narrow set of meanings to his work. If Lichtenstein's work came to be identified as Pop, that label has often obscured those very features that differentiate his project from the work of other artists in the movement. In light of this, the current exhibition – by bringing together a large body of works by the artist – offers us the opportunity to examine Lichtenstein's practice in its own right. An examination of his particular approach to the broader techniques and themes treated by the movement can help us distinguish his version of Pop Art from the work of his contemporaries. The meaning of Lichtenstein's work of the early 1960s is not limited to its treatment of commercial subject matter or to its artistic adaptation of mechanical techniques. Rather, his work also consistently returns us to issues of looking and vision; through his art Lichtenstein considered how commercial culture and mechanical reproduction have affected the basic matter of how we see.

The diverse practices of the individual Pop artists were often linked in the early 1960s through their common focus on the consumer object. Their interest in the object was spurred in part by the slightly earlier artistic projects of Jasper Johns and Robert Rauschenberg who, in their work of the 1950s, had employed conventional symbols, common objects and vernacular materials (for this reason the two have often been referred to as proto-Pop artists). Johns and Rauschenberg were concerned in part with investigating the legacy of Marcel Duchamp's concept of the readymade. Decades earlier Duchamp had initiated the radical project of choosing common, industrially-produced objects (a bottle dryer, a snow shovel) and designating them works of art solely by virtue of the artist's act of selection. The legacy of the Duchampian readymade was reinvigorated through Pop, whether in Andy Warhol's paintings that featured re-

Tire. 1962
Oil on canvas
68 x 58 inches / 173 x 148 cm
The Museum of Modern Art, New York
Fractional gift of Mr. and Mrs. Donald G. Fisher

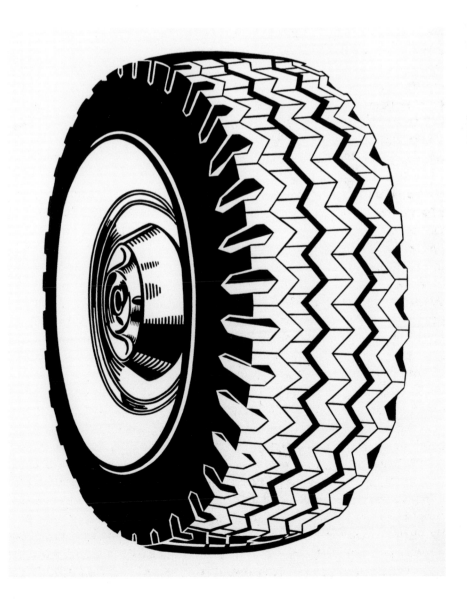

peated rows of mass-produced objects (such as Coca-Cola bottles and Campbell's soup cans); Tom Wesselmann's oversized consumerist still-life collages; or Claes Oldenburg's sculptural transformations of industrial objects into soft, biomorphic forms (Oldenburg's *Soft Toilet* of 1966 makes direct reference to Duchamp's infamous 1917 *Fountain*, a common urinal displayed as a work of art). Early exhibitions featuring the work of these artists (such as *New Paintings of Common Objects* and *Six Painters and the Object*) repeatedly emphasized the movement's orientation toward the object.[2]

Lichtenstein's work was no exception to this tendency; it was through paintings like *Radio*, 1961, *Golf Ball*, 1962, and *Tire,* 1962, that critics aligned him with other practitioners of Pop Art. Nevertheless, his approach to the object is distinctive. For one, in Lichtenstein's work the object is presented as a singular, iconic unit, in contrast to the manifold repetitions employed by an artist like Warhol. By isolating the object in this way – and by graphically simplifying it and presenting it in stark black and white – Lichtenstein turns the act of depiction into an exercise in abstract form. Many of his paintings of objects veer toward abstraction, whether *Golf Ball*'s radiating field of arcs enclosed within a circular form or the pattern of bold, repeated chevrons in *Tire*. In this way these works often make reference to the traditions of abstract painting. For instance, critics have long noted that the arcing lines of *Golf Ball* bear more than a passing resemblance to the distinctive forms used in Piet Mondrian's plus-and-minus paintings.[3] Taking on some of the central concerns of modernist abstraction, Lichtenstein often sets up in these paintings a visual tension between figure and ground. For example, *Golf Ball* offers a veritable oscillation between the figural resolution of the object and its dissolution into the blank ground, in part because the white of the ball is the same as that of the background. In other words, although we tend to perceive the depicted image as an object – in this case, a golf ball – at the same time we are aware of it as an utterly flat field of abstracted marks.

Lichtenstein's graphic simplification of the image is not, however, the only thing that sets his consumer objects apart from those of his Pop colleagues. He also consistently removed any identifiable brand names, trademarks and product logos from his paintings.[4] Lichtenstein's approach to Pop Art is vastly different from that of Warhol, whose work consistently reiterates the significance of the brand name – whether in his *Campbell's Soup Can* and *Coca-Cola Bottle* paintings or in his *Brillo Box* sculptures. Warhol uses the product logo to call our attention to the repetition and standardization of the commodity form. Even Warhol's star portraits – such as the *Marilyn* paintings – show how the celebrity's persona assumes many of the same characteristics as the packaged consumer object. Yet in Lichtenstein's work we are given no access to the consumerist world of trademarked goods; he gives us, not brand name items, but rather such generic images as *Golf Ball, Radio* and *Tire*. In much the same way that Lichtenstein isolates the object on a singular canvas, he isolates his work from the very identifying elements that would otherwise link it to the real-world circulation of commodities. Our understanding of this characteristic of Lichtenstein's work challenges conventional readings of Pop Art as a simple mirror of consumer culture, in that it demonstrates the complexity – and ambivalence – that attended the artist's engagement with the common object.

One of Lichtenstein's most profound contributions to Pop Art was his transformation of the codes of cartooning into a viable formal language for painting.[5] A classic Pop canvas like *Masterpiece*, 1962, contains all the basic elements of Lichtenstein's trademark style: the use of bold black outlines (note particularly the line that traces the silhouetted profile of the male figure); the reduction of the painter's palette to black, white and the primary colours (red, yellow and blue); and the use of areas of regularized dots that imitate – in enlarged form – the halftone dot screens of mechanical printing. As in the best of his Pop paintings, Lichtenstein employs these devices here to profound formal effect. For instance, he sets dotted areas against passages of monochrome colour, as in the dotted face and neck of the female figure juxtaposed with the bright red of her shirt and yellow of her hair (each of these areas, in turn, is outlined by a bold black line). Or he uses the word balloon above, not simply as a space for text, but as a distinct, almost collage-like element in its own right. By using such diverse formal strategies Lichtenstein offers, in an otherwise flat image, a vibrant and complex play of visual textures. Nevertheless, the formal inventiveness of the artist's chosen pictorial vocabulary cannot be separated from its technological associations. Lichtenstein's reduction of his painterly vocabulary to a set of highly structured and mechanically derived codes is an insistent reminder of the rationalization of vision in a culture of mechanical reproduction. As such, the fields of regularized dots in the artist's paintings should not be taken as referring solely to the dot-screens of the mechanically printed page; these are signs of the standardization of visual data understood more broadly, as in the pixilation of the image on the television screen or computer display.

Considering the consistency with which Lichtenstein was concerned in his work with issues of vision, it should come as no surprise that acts of seeing and looking are frequently foregrounded in his paintings. This is true even from the very beginning of his experimentation with the Pop idiom, in such canvases as *Look Mickey* and *I Can See the Whole Room…And There's Nobody In It!*, both from 1961. The titles of these works – with their references to looking and seeing – already signal the artist's concern with acts of vision, and the scenes depicted in these paintings bear this out. *Look Mickey* describes a veritable circuit of looks: Donald Duck gazes into the water below while

Bratatat! 1962
Oil on canvas. 46 x 34 inches / 117 x 86 cm
Private Collection

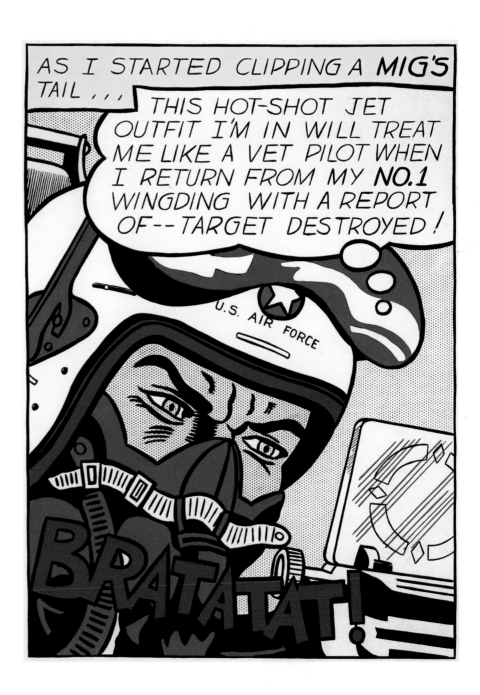

Mickey Mouse looks at him from behind, covering his mouth in a gesture that signifies a stifled laugh. In *I Can See the Whole Room* a male figure stares out at us from the painting, his face and hand framed by a circular peephole that visually rhymes with his single exposed eye. These images take up a longstanding tradition in the history of art that prompts us to reflect on the very activity – looking – in which we as viewers are engaged. In other Pop works Lichtenstein was not concerned solely with vision alone. A good number of the artist's paintings from the period – particularly his well-known images derived from war comic books – depict interactions between human vision and machines. In these works Lichtenstein depicted human figures looking through mechanical viewing devices, whether the cockpit gun sight in a painting like *Bratatat!*, 1963, or the submarine periscope of *Torpedo...Los!*, 1963.[6] In these paintings form and subject converge; the artist's depiction of the technological augmentation of vision is offered in a pictorial language that – as discussed above – calls our attention to the mechanical standardization of the visual field.

In spite of the fact that Lichtenstein is most readily identified as a Pop artist, his passage through Pop was upon reflection rather brief, just four or five years in a career that spanned decades. He soon moved on to other subject matter, whether in the deadpan parodies of gestural painting in the *Brushstroke* canvases or in the near-abstractions of the *Mirror* paintings. Take, as an example, *Mirror #1* from 1966; although he derived the initial motif from a printed image in a commercial brochure, Lichtenstein disengages the depiction from its commercial origins and pushes it toward a more extreme level of abstraction.[7] Yet at the same time in *Mirror #1* he continues to work through many of the concerns central to his exploration of Pop: he produces a vibrant repertory of forms out of a simplified pictorial language; appropriates commercial imagery and expands on its possible range of meanings; and confronts the experience of – and the limits to – vision (*Mirror #1*, after all, offers the promise of a reflection that is never fulfilled). Late in the "What is Pop Art?" interview, Gene Swenson asked Lichtenstein if he thought Pop Art would attain a universal influence. The artist answered: "I don't know. I doubt it. It seems too particular – too much the expression of a few personalities. Pop might be a difficult starting point for a painter. He would have great difficulty in making these brittle images yield to compositional purposes..."[8] Faced with the difficulty that Pop Art presented for a painter, Lichtenstein doubted it would go on to have a universal influence. From our own retrospective view, with the enduring legacy of the artist's work in mind, we can safely say that on this point Lichtenstein would eventually prove himself wrong.

Michael Lobel received his PhD in Art History from Yale University in 1999 and is the author of *Image Duplicator: Roy Lichtenstein and the Emergence of Pop Art* (Yale University Press, 2002). He is assistant professor of art history at Bard College. He has been the recipient of numerous academic honors, including a Henry Luce Foundation/ACLS Doctoral Dissertation Fellowship in American Art and postdoctoral fellowships at the Getty Research Institute and the Smithsonian Institution.

1   Roy Lichtenstein, as quoted in Gene R. Swenson, "What is Pop Art? Answers from Eight Painters, Part I," *Art News* 62, no. 7 (November 1963), p. 25

2   *New Paintings of Common Objects* was a 1962 exhibition at the Pasadena Art Museum curated by Walter Hopps. *Six Painters and the Object* curated by Lawrence Alloway, showed in 1963 at the Guggenheim Museum in New York.

3   Diane Waldman first made this connection in her essay for Lichtenstein's 1969 retrospective at the Guggenheim Museum; see Diane Waldman, *Roy Lichtenstein*, Solomon R. Guggenheim Museum, New York, 1969, p. 15

4   There is one early painting by Lichtenstein – *Roto-Broil* – that features a brand name, but it is the exception that defines the rule; after that point Lichtenstein left off brand names, product logos and trademarks from his depictions of consumer objects

5   For more on this point see Kirk Varnedoe and Adam Gopnik, *High and Low: Modern Art and Popular Culture*, MoMA, New York, 1990, p. 199-206

6   For more on the representation of technologized vision in Lichtenstein's Pop work, see Chapter Three ("Technology Envisioned: Lichtenstein's Monocularity") in Michael Lobel, *Image Duplicator: Roy Lichtenstein and the Emergence of Pop Art*, New Haven, 2002, pp. 75-103.

7   For the source image and discussion of *Mirror #1*, see Diane Waldman, *Roy Lichtenstein*, Solomon R. Guggenheim Museum, New York, 1993, pp. 183-9

8   Lichtenstein in Swenson, "What is Pop Art?", p. 63

Torpedo ... Los! 1963
Oil on canvas. 68 x 80 inches / 173 x 203 cm
Private Collection

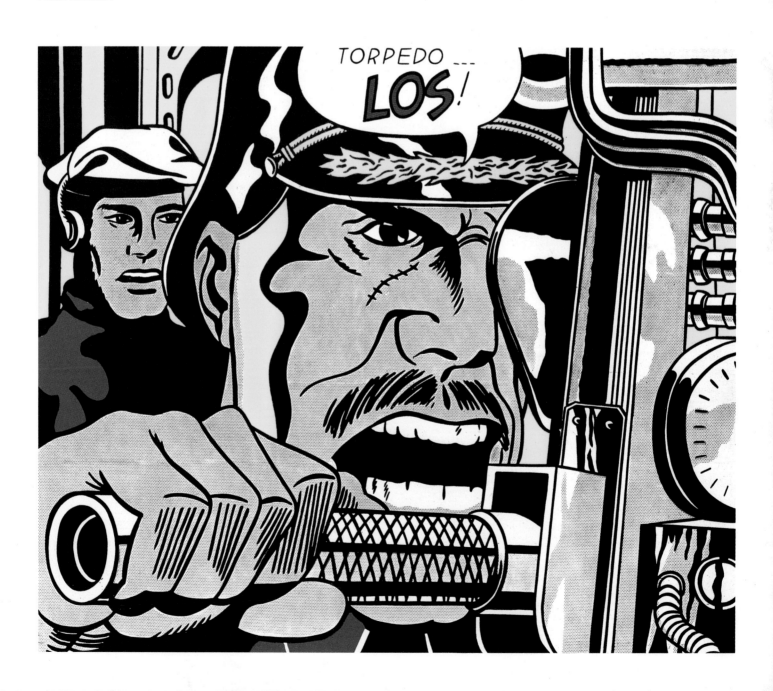

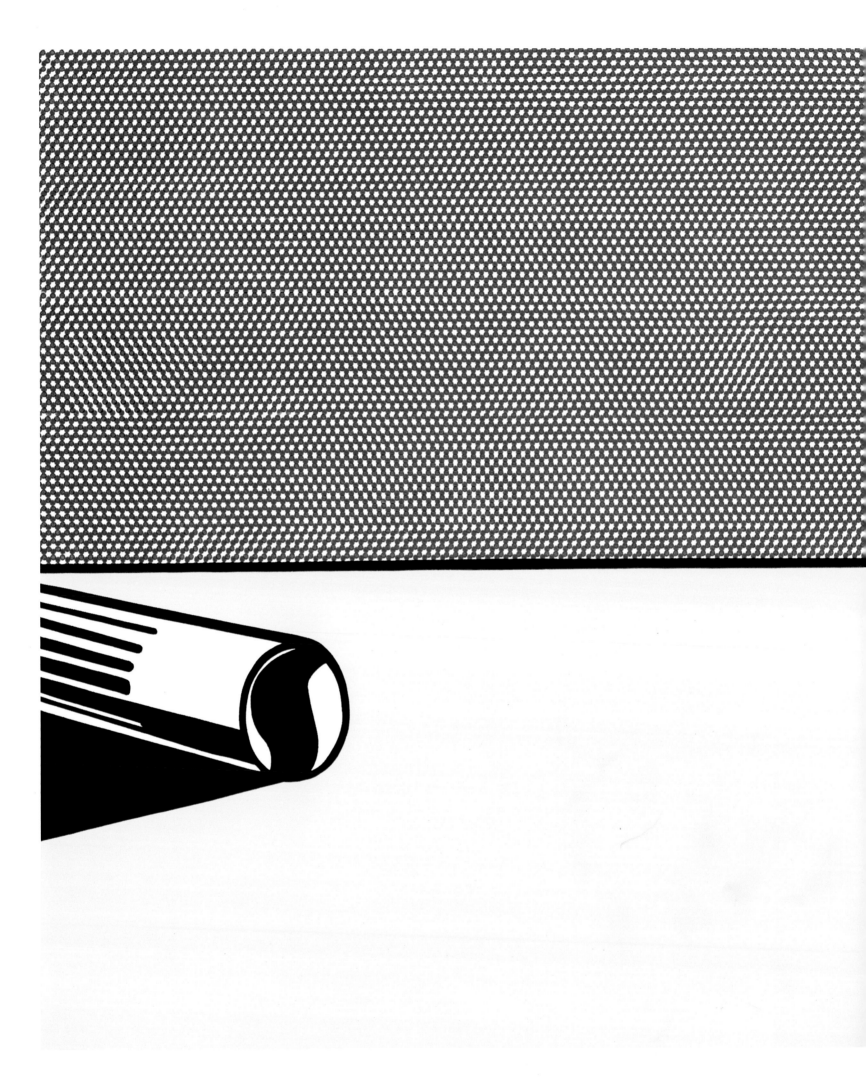

25.
Landscape with Column. 1965
Private Collection

21.
Sussex. 1964
Robert and Jane Rosenblum, N.Y.

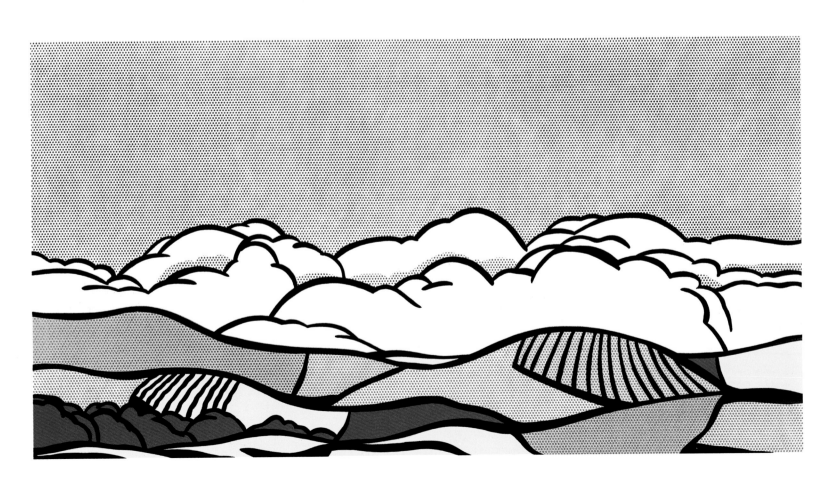

28.
Yellow Sky. 1966
Ulmer Museum, Stiftung Sammlung Kurt Fried

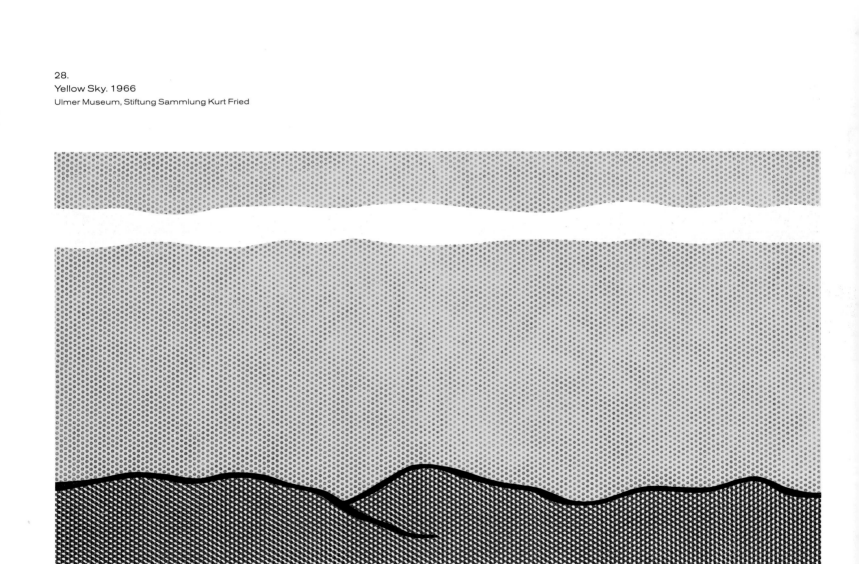

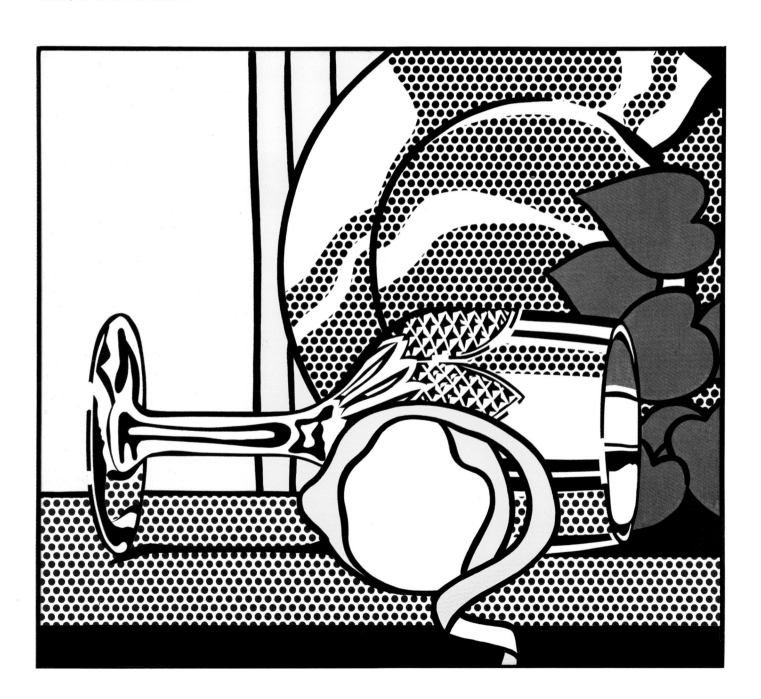

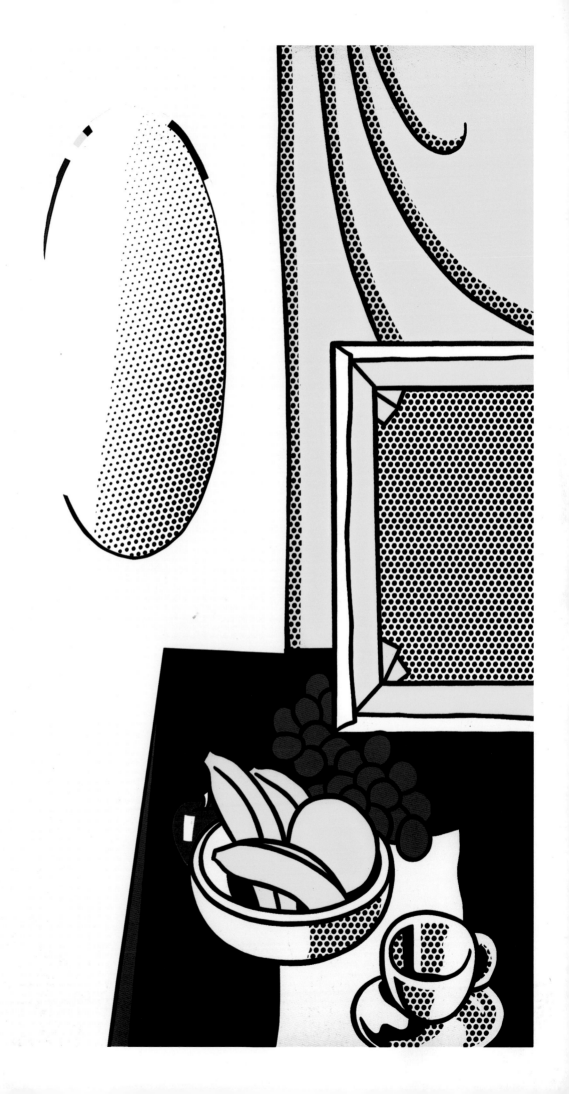

33.
Still Life with Mirror. 1972
Private Collection

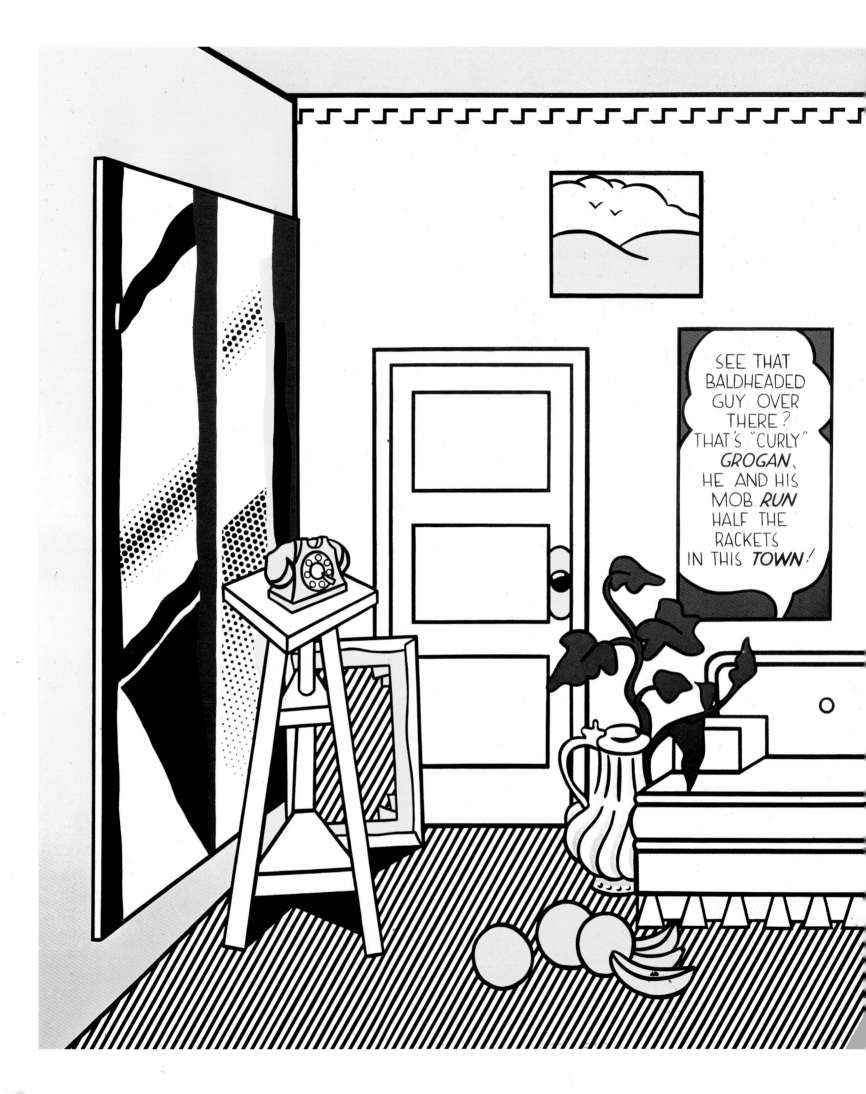

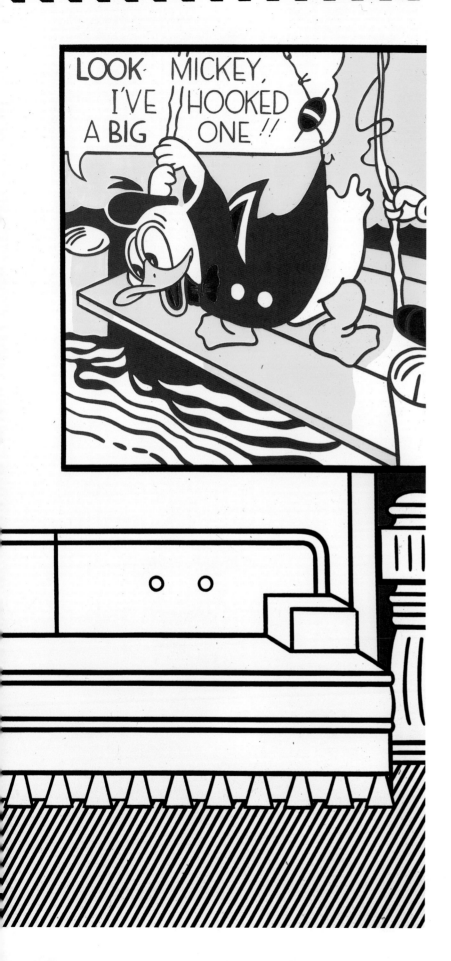

35.
Artist's Studio No. 1 (Look Mickey). 1973
Collection Walker Art Center, Minneapolis

36.
Still Life with Swiss Cheese. 1973
David Lichtenstein

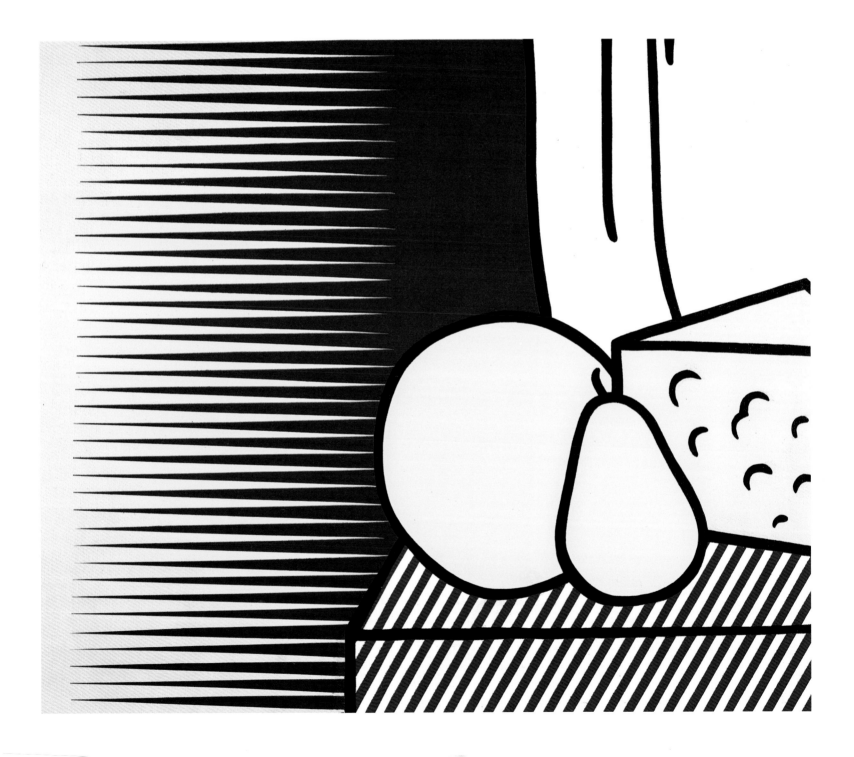

41.
Girl with Tear III. 1977
Fondation Beyeler, Riehen/Basel

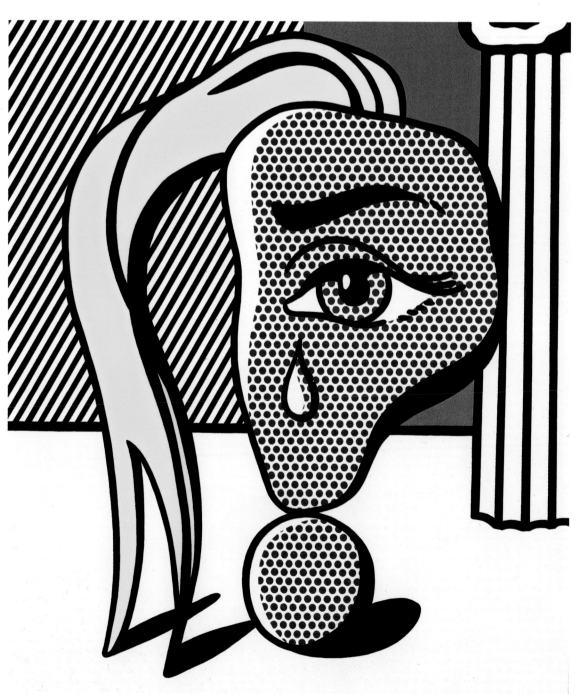

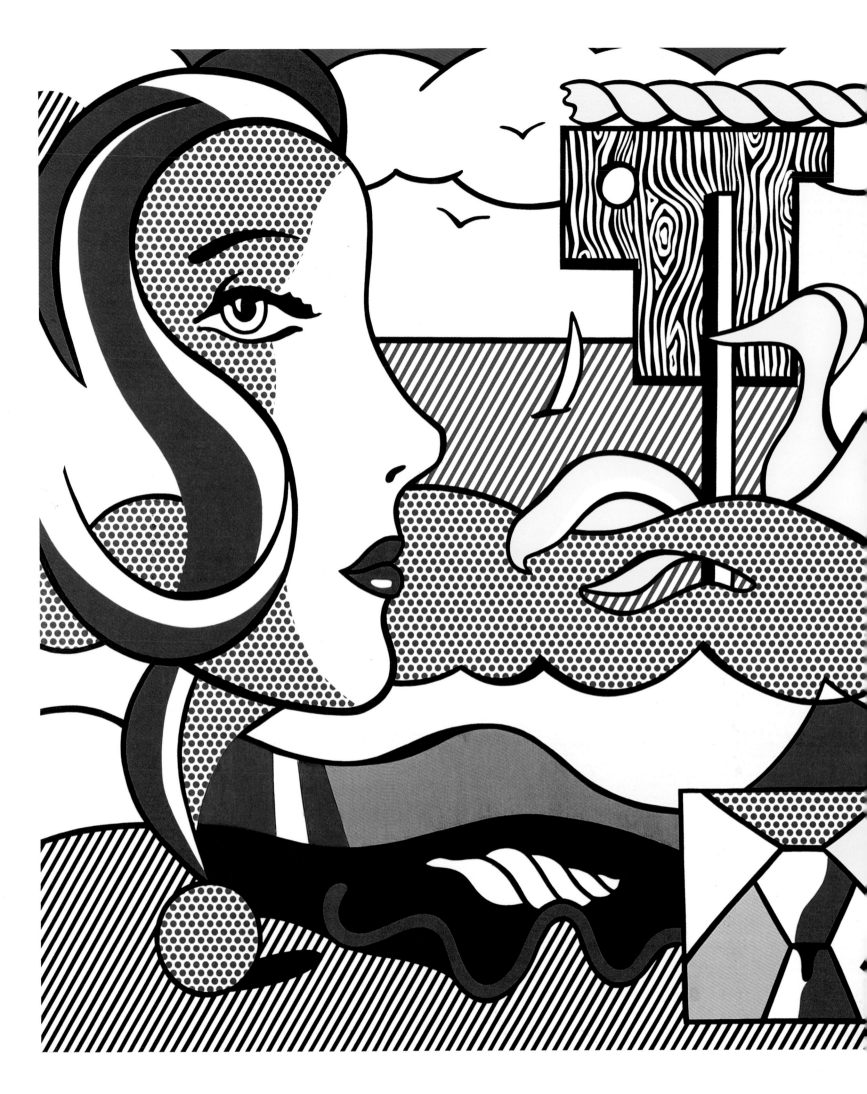

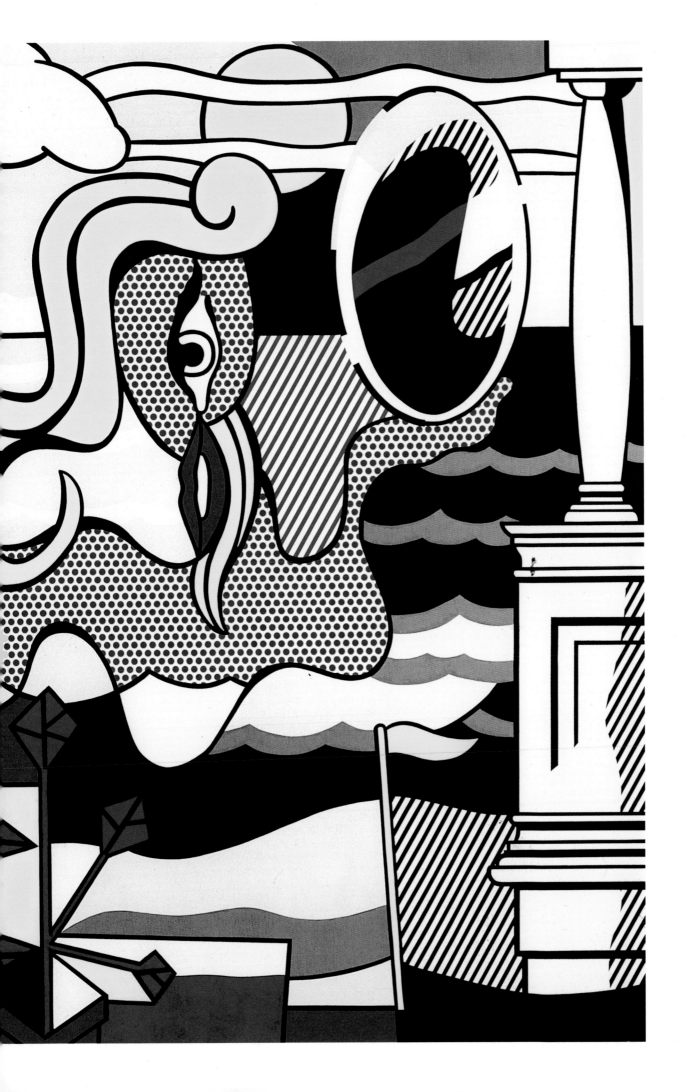

40.
Figures in
Landscape. 1977
Louisiana Museum
of Modern Art

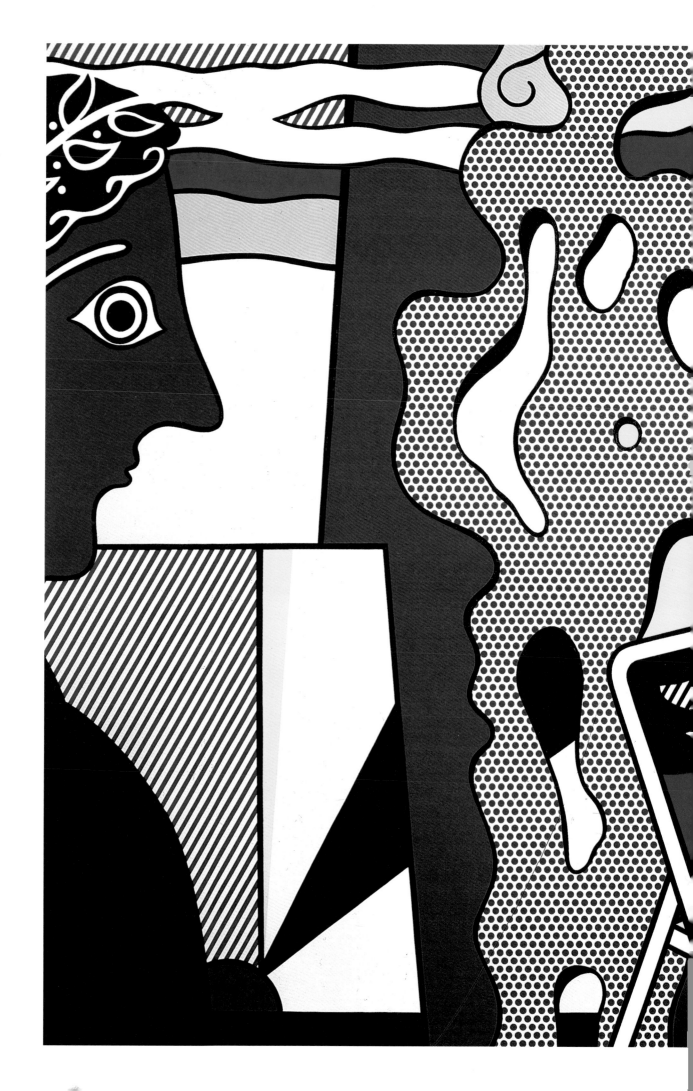

43.
Cosmology. 1978
Private Collection

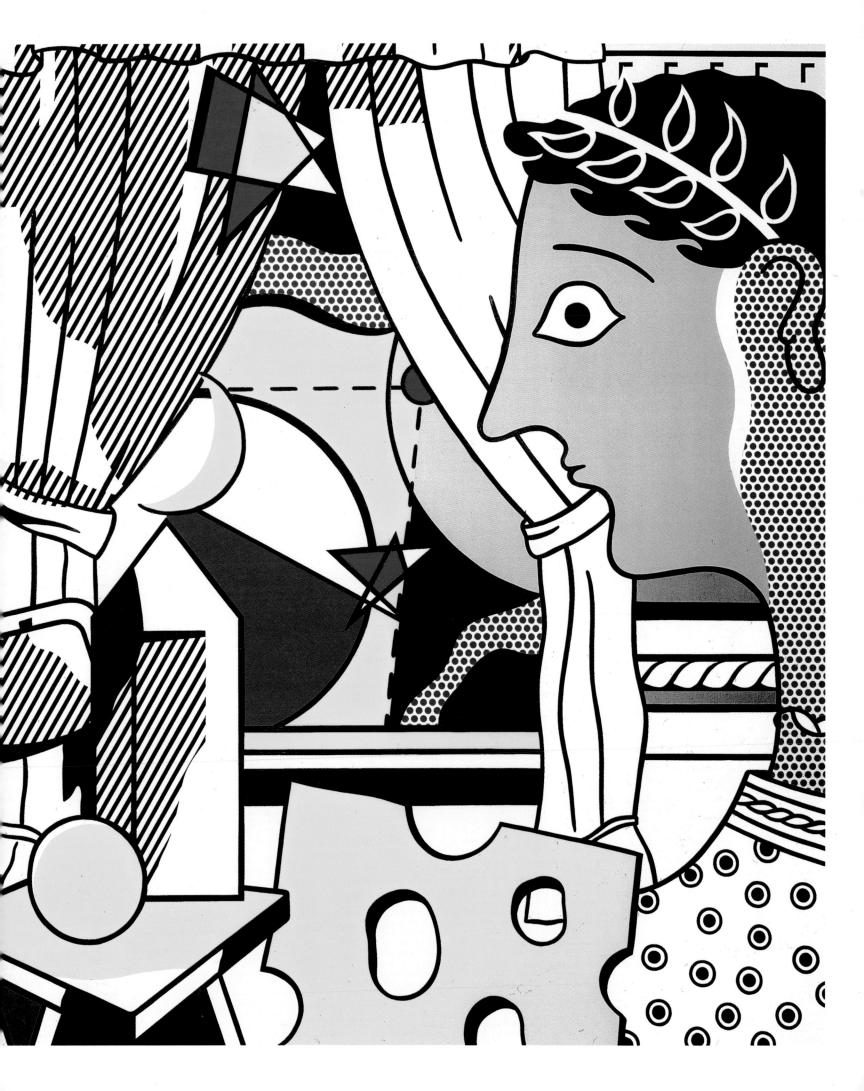

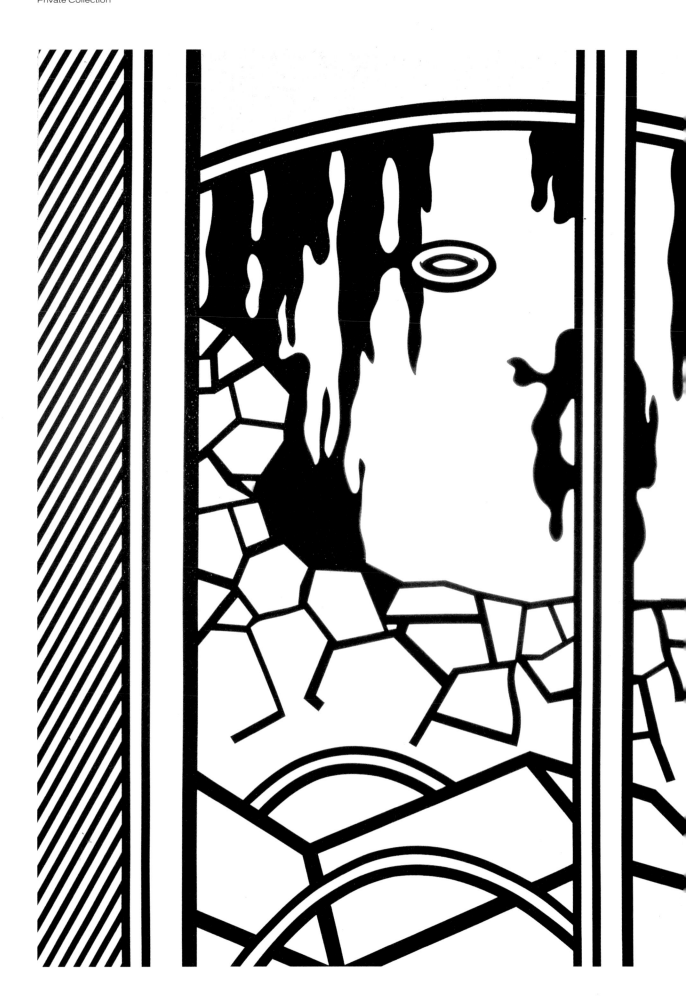

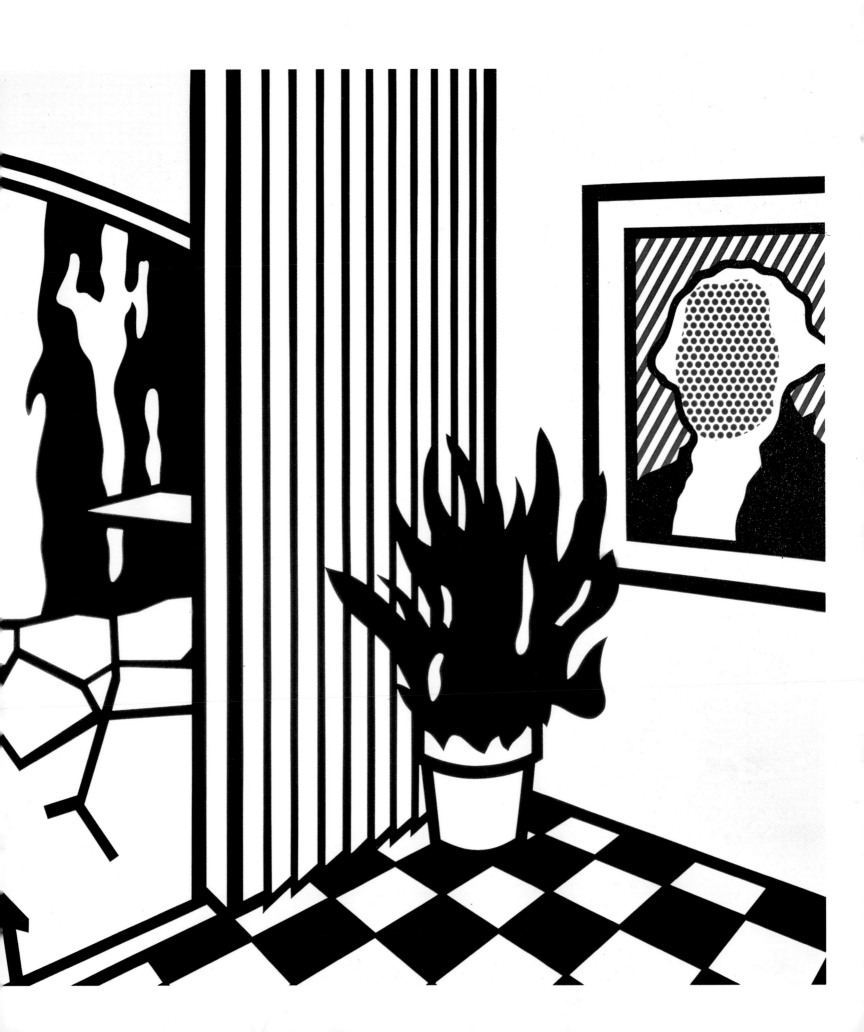

50.
Interior with Motel Room Painting. 1992
Private Collection

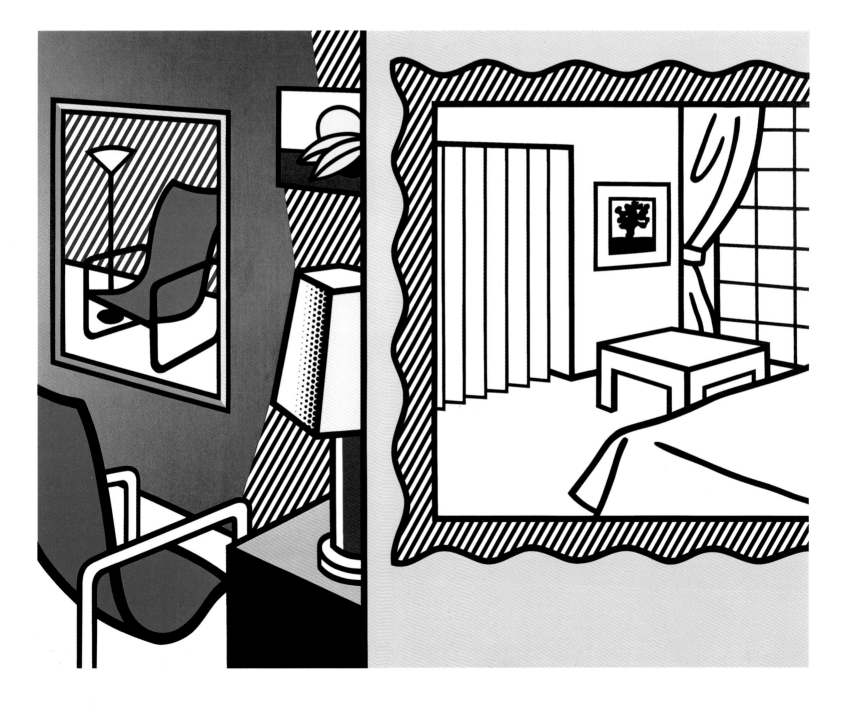

51.
Landscape in Fog. 1996
Private Collection

54.
Vista with Bridge. 1996
Private Collection

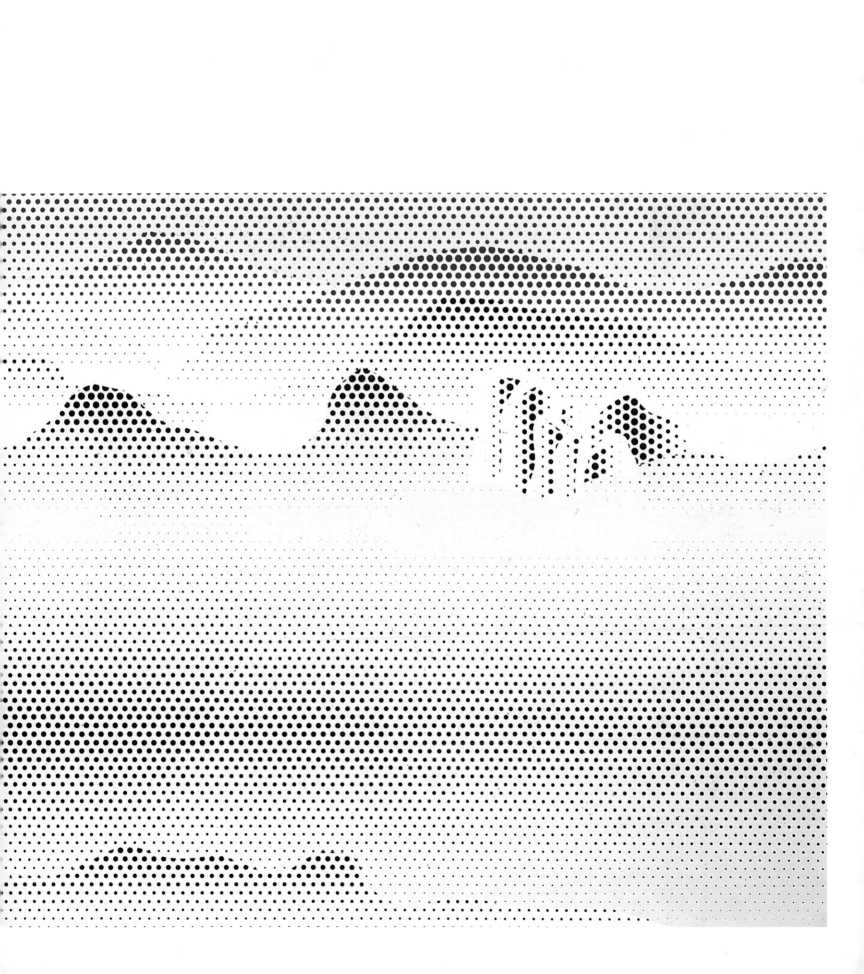

52.
Landscape with Boat. 1996
Private Collection

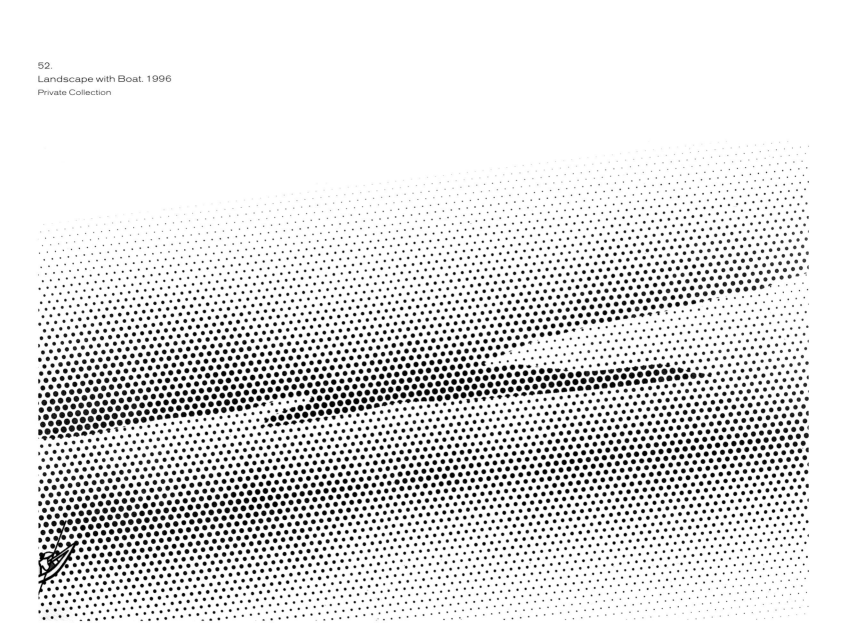

53.
Tall Mountains. 1996
Private Collection

55.
Interior with Painting of Bather. 1997
The Eli and Edythe L. Broad Collection

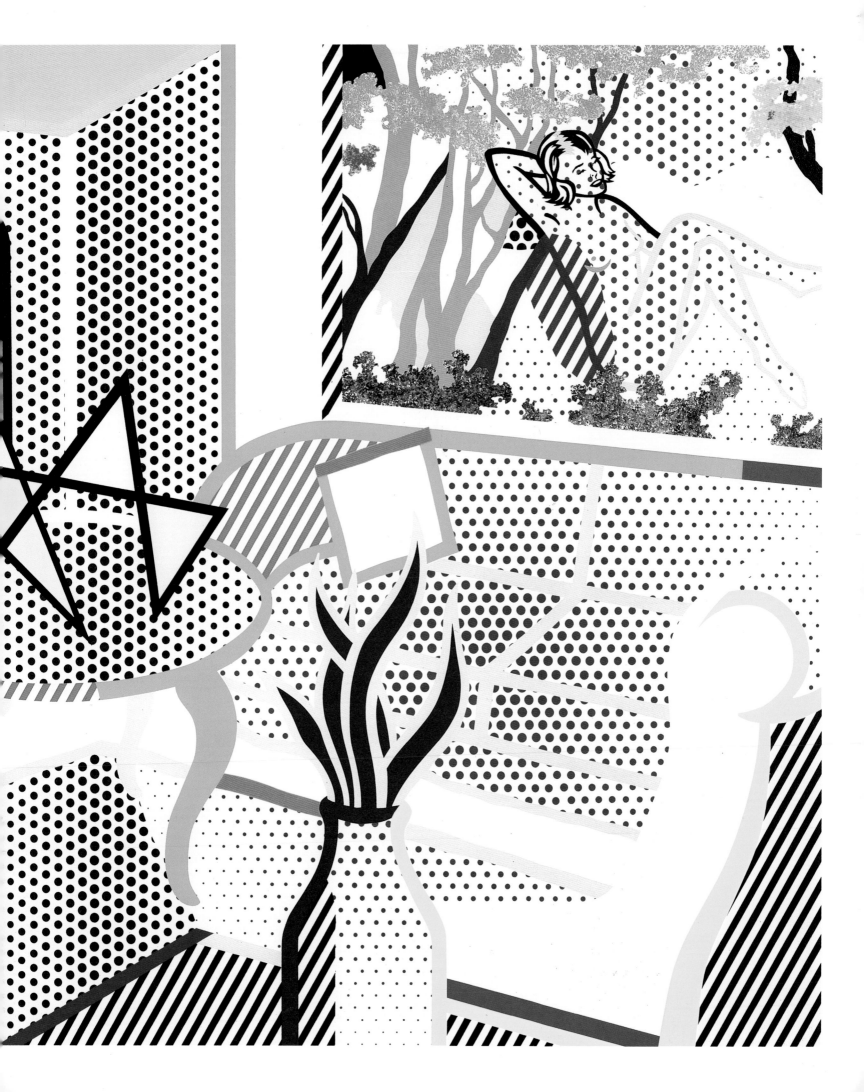

Jack Cowart

More Than Meets the Eye

One of the several charter purposes of the Roy Lichtenstein Foundation is to conduct research on the artist's life and art. Central to this are our current catalogue raisonné project (eventually to issue in seven volumes, each one taking many years to complete accurately), an oral history project and a photographic archive project searching all known images of the artist and his studios.

On the occasion of this European retrospective, we are pleased to publish preliminary information relating to two of these Foundation projects. Avis Berman's oral history interview excerpts focus on Roy Lichtenstein's complex early career up to 1961 – that breakthrough, contradictory and evolutionary year in the history of Pop Art and the life of this artist. Woven through the oral history is a carefully selected survey of historic images of Lichtenstein and his surroundings researched and selected by our photo-archivist, Clare Bell.

In general, researchers and the public have yet to appreciate the full picture of Roy Lichtenstein's deep pre-existing intellectual and visual interest in newspaper, comic, and popular culture images, his fascination with illustrational systems of signs and symbols, and his wondering, inquisitive interest in trying to figure how the mind understands what the eyes perceive. These interests clearly emerge as early as the mid-1940s, and Roy would produce almost five hundred ambitious and individual works of art before 1961. Thus Lichtenstein's creative explosion of 1961 was years in the making. He already had his artistic eye, skill and 'voice', but what he then found were viable universal subjects worthy of his interest and re-creation.

Of course, what Lichtenstein did achieve in 1961 is and remains legitimately stunning. During the last six or eight months of 1961, he created at least thirty paintings and sixteen finished drawings, many of which will remain an active repertoire of Pop subject-types for much of his subsequent career.

His was not some spontaneous conversion but it was a time when Lichtenstein took huge risks and found a critical new Pop idiom. And with enough public response to these works after a decade of many gallery exhibitions but only modest sales Lichtenstein became a hot item, with a hot dealer, and evolved as a New York insider of the hot new art and culture wave of the ecstatic, fame-oriented Sixties.

At this time he resolved and radicalized his technical rendering technique, method and scale. He devised a stripped down scheme that could be endlessly, subtly, adaptable. It was a practical discipline as he fully committed to ubiquitous Benday dots and the fluid black outline, with a restricted four-colour palette (red, black, blue, yellow on a white background). He quickly evolved a curious, subversive and quite malleable, almost 'blank,' oddball and consciously 'dumb', but engaging, surrealist variants of objects. Taken from commercial and popular illustrations, these images seemed realistic and accessible to the public, despite the high level of inherent abstraction. This contradiction intrigued the artist.

"Roy is always Roy" and both these earlier works and their successive switches back and forth between figuration and abstraction are prototypes for the underlying themes of his many later Pop works and processes continuing throughout his career.

We remind those who think the birth of American Pop Art and Roy Lichtenstein is defined and all wrapped up, or those who like their art history crisp and simple, that, quite to the contrary, the real 1961 story for Lichtenstein and many other artists of his generation has yet to be written.

Jack Cowart is Executive Director of the Lichtenstein Foundation and has a PhD in history of art from The Johns Hopkins University, 1972. Most recently he was deputy Director/Chief Curator of the Corcoran Gallery of Art (1992-1999) and Head of the Department of 20th Century Art at the National Gallery of Art (1983-1992).

Roy Lichtenstein in his studio in Columbus, Ohio, ca. 1949
Photographer unknown. Courtesy Roy Lichtenstein Foundation Archives

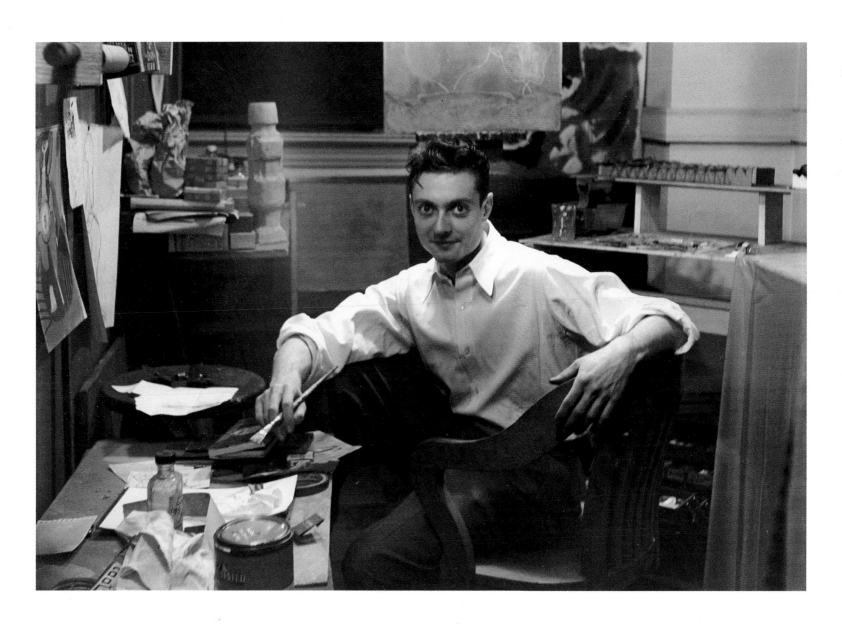

Avis Berman

The Transformations of Roy Lichtenstein:
an oral history

In 1962 or 1963, when I was visiting Roy in New Jersey, he said, "I'm amazed. People knock at the front door, and in a very angry manner, say, 'Tell me how you did it.' You know? 'Tell me how you did it. Why are you successful and I've been beating my head against my studio wall all these years?'" And he'd say, "Come in. I just did it. It just happened."
— Sidney Chafetz[1]

In 1961, Roy Lichtenstein (1923-1997) produced the first fully realized paintings featuring the style, source material and repertoire of motifs that he would investigate for the rest of his life. His principal imagery was lifted from comic strips and print advertisements, and the canvases resulting from them were executed in black-and-white, in emulation of the illustrations in the newspapers, magazines and telephone books from which they were drawn, or they were restricted to a palette of bright primaries. Most famously, he appropriated the Benday dots, the minute mechanical patterning used in commercial engraving, to convey texture and gradations of colour. The dots became a trademark device forever identified with Lichtenstein and Pop Art, the movement he helped originate.

Although Lichtenstein was a classicist dedicated to the witty exploration of how we see, discussions of his work often became fixated on the subject matter and its commercial sources because they upended every reigning prejudice known to high art. He celebrated yet debunked the glorious dumbness of everyday American things, but through a highly formalist filter. Alvin Katz, one of Lichtenstein's college classmates, recalled that he had adopted this approach as a student. Lichtenstein once said to him,

The only thing I remember really being interested in was that it was confounding as to why one set of lines – somebody's drawings – was considered brilliant, and somebody's else's, that may have looked better to you, was considered nothing by almost everyone.[2]

Lichtenstein expressed the same view to the painter Joseph O'Sickey, whom he met in the late 1940s:

We went to New York and toured the galleries one Saturday, and it was all Abstract Expressionist, everything, and Roy said, "I guess you can't do that any longer." And I said, "No, we can't do that. The best thing for me to do is go and paint the back yard," and he said he was going to do something else. "And most of the painting doesn't work anyway." (Roy and I saw most Abstract Expressionism itself as subject matter, and only a few artists as expressive.) So we were pointing out why they didn't work, and what was wrong with the paintings. As we went through the galleries, he said, "You know, the trouble is, people can't tell the difference." When he started doing the Pop Art he said, "You know, they're so subject matter-oriented, they really can't tell a good drawing from a bad drawing. The thing to do is take bad drawings and make good ones out of them." He said the worst drawings he could find were in the telephone book.[3]

In the words of the artist's wife, Dorothy Lichtenstein, a painting's external form was not important to him:

Roy saw himself as an abstract artist in that he felt there was such a thing as unification that you could do on the canvas – it could be one mark and it would either have it or not ... in order to make something new, the style or the look of it was important, but after you decided what that was going to be, it really didn't matter at all ... His subject matter

114

is so strong that it's hard to say that he could avoid it, but he did it as much as he could. [4]

Another reason why Lichtenstein did not place much weight on subject matter is that he had found the germ of it so early in his career without extraordinary results. Paraphrasing, particularly the paraphrasing of despised images, was the most consistent theme of Lichtenstein's work for 45 years. Sidney Chafetz, who met Lichtenstein in 1948, recalled: "In 1951, he was working from nineteenth-century American painting." Asked why Lichtenstein would have turned to what was then an outlandish source of inspiration, Chafetz said:

I think it was part of Roy's wit. He found something intriguing about the nineteenth-century historical painting. He thought there was something humorous in the innocence of the representation.

I think Roy was always searching. He was looking for something that other people were not. The common imagery never interested him … [H]e had a very high level of curiosity, and he had a sly approach to looking at history. [5]

There were a number of tantalizing clues of what was to come, from humorous images of George Washington painted in 1950 and 1951 to *Ten Dollar Bill*, a 1956 lithograph that has attained a special status as Lichtenstein's first proto-Pop work. Lichtenstein himself acknowledged it as a milestone, according to Letty Lou Eisenhauer, who met him in 1961:

I have a print of the "Ten Dollar Bill" that he did … I always used to laugh and say, "You did it way before Andy. Way before Andy [Warhol]." He liked that idea. He wasn't going to hide it. He understood that, and thought it was wonderful … that he had done a ten-dollar bill a long time ago. [6]

As early as 1957 or 1958, sketchy portraits of Mickey Mouse and Donald Duck appeared in charcoal drawings and on canvas even while Lichtenstein was experimenting with a fully abstract style dependent on waves of dramatic brushstrokes – another mannerism he would lovingly satirize in a few years. These images of dollars and ducks, of Indians and airplanes, though flavored with characteristic Lichtenstein humour, were hesitant in presentation and remained painterly, expressionist and tasteful. He had to arrive at the crucial insight of removing the artiness from the art, of realizing that the truest innocence of representation lay in mimicking the numb affect of the cartoon as much as its characters. Ivan Karp, who would rescue Lichtenstein from obscurity in his capacity as director of the Leo Castelli Gallery, summarized the artist's earlier career in New York, saying, "Lichtenstein had three one-man shows at the Heller Gallery [in 1952, 1953, and 1957]. They were comparatively sedate, semi-cubist kind of paintings with little intimations of cartoons." [7]

Lichtenstein cheerfully admitted that his metamorphosis from prosaic abstract painter into someone who blatantly questioned the nature of art with work that "had every quality that Abstract Expressionism eschewed" [8] had the appearance of a miraculous event. He credited the magical trajectory of his career to his landing at Douglass College, the women's division of Rutgers University, in 1960. There, sur-

rounded by free-thinking artists like Allan Kaprow, Geoffrey Hendricks, George Segal, Robert Watts, Robert Whitman, and Lucas Samaras, Lichtenstein blossomed in an environment of excitement and experiment. [9] And when he galvanized the art-public after his first one-person show at the Leo Castelli Gallery in February 1962, Lichtenstein was scorned as an overnight success, a wallower in meretricious celebrity whose triumph was neither deserved nor earned, as Sidney Chafetz's testimony, quoted above, makes clear. Both consciously and unconsciously Lichtenstein subscribed to this apprehension of himself as the sensation of the moment. Until the mid-1980s he could not believe that the fame and adulation would last, but for the opposite reason – unlike his detractors, he knew how long it had taken him to find his way to a transfiguring idiom.

No one doubts that the atmosphere at Rutgers University catalyzed Lichtenstein's development as an artist, but his accident of fortune was prepared for by steady training and craft. He had been painting, sculpting and drawing seriously for two decades; he worked ceaselessly, sometimes against heavy odds, and never gave up on building an exhibition record in New York. He had hung in and hung on, though he took care that few glimpsed the fingernail marks.

Once Lichtenstein achieved his signature style, he had little interest in dwelling on earlier, less resolved paintings or on the painful aspects of his past life, which included a first marriage that ended in 1965. He maintained strict control over the discourse about his work, his polite amiability veiling a stance that revealed the minimum of information about inner intent to journalists, historians, curators and critics. The earlier pictures were largely suppressed, and iconographical continuities, emotional conflicts, or autobiographical content inherent in the Pop pieces were not probed. In the latter, Lichenstein encouraged inquiries centered on the psychologically safer operation of pinpointing superficial similarities and differences between the comic book and commercial illustrations and the paintings they spawned.

The received opinion surrounding Roy Lichtenstein's brilliant debut has remained static because not enough written documentation exists to counteract or amplify it. Lichtenstein did not enjoy correspondence, and by the 1960s, the telephone had replaced the letter as a primary means of communication. As a young artist-teacher, Lichtenstein tended to throw out old records when he moved. He demonstrated no impulse to preserve or accumulate papers.

The Roy Lichtenstein Foundation, which was established by the artist's family after his death, is strongly archival in orientation. It is soliciting and creating salient primary documents that will guide critics, art historians and other interpreters of Lichtenstein's art. In particular, the necessity arose to initiate an oral history project on Roy Lichtenstein's life and times precisely because the artist had obscured his pre-Pop career so effectively. A beginning narrative of Roy Lichtenstein's development, culminating in the breakthrough of the early 1960s, lends itself to a documentary-biographical vehicle like the oral history precisely because so much of that journey was dependent on a densely-layered palimpsest of friendships, collaborations, and interrelationships. In the text that follows, based mainly on interviews conducted for the Roy Lichtenstein Foundation, I have concentrated on the verbatim testimony elicited and kept my own annotations sparse. Where necessary, I have included similar or jarring accounts of the same event, either to corroborate what happened or to accentuate the *Rashomon*-like nature of individual memory, of which all readers must be wary.

Born and raised in New York City, Roy Lichtenstein entered Ohio State University in 1940 as a fine arts major. He was mesmerized by the teaching of Hoyt L. Sherman, whom he maintained was the person who showed him how to see and whose perception-based approach to art affected him for the rest of his life. The artist Chuck Csuri, who was both an undergraduate and graduate student with Lichtenstein, recalled:

We both felt … that Sherman's conception of visual form … was a better theory than most other people around us. We were very strong formalists in those days, and when we would look at drawings and paintings, we'd talk about them in terms of visual structure, in terms of figure-ground relationships, in terms of coincidence of edge, in terms of whether or not it had some of the characteristics of a Cézanne drawing or painting. [We singled out Cézanne] because Cézanne gave attention to the picture plane – the shape, the kinds of theories that had to do with formal structure and colour relationships. And Cézanne … was the springboard into Cubism. [10]

In 1966, the British critic David Sylvester asked Lichtenstein what he considered to be the main sources of his art, and the artist replied, "I think the aesthetic influence on me is probably more Cubism than anything. I think even the cartoons themselves are influenced by Cubism, because the hard-edged character which is brought about by the printing creates a kind of cubist look which perhaps wasn't intended." [11]

Lichtenstein's undergraduate education was interrupted when he was drafted into the U.S. Army in 1943. After the Second World War ended, he returned to the university to finish his B.F.A. degree. While working on an M.F.A. at Ohio State, he was also made an instructor in the Fine Arts department. In June 1949, he married Isabel Wilson (1921-1980), who worked in a cooperative art gallery in Cleveland. Although Lichtenstein's paintings and prints – intimate works in the vein of Paul Klee that poked lyrical fun at medieval knights, castles and maidens – were not advanced compared to contemporaneous works being produced by the New York School, their faux-primitive whimsy impressed his colleagues in Ohio, and they regarded him as a talented artist with an unusual vision.

Sidney Chafetz: *Roy's personality was one of quiet sophistication. Roy was a New York boy. Most of the faculty at the time were Ohio boys, but Roy had already seen a great deal of the world of art. Most of us had come out of World War II experiences, but Roy, in his own quiet way, was really very much respected by all of his peers. His shyness disappeared at faculty parties, where he could sit down at a party and play a mean boogie-woogie on the piano, and really be the life of the party.*

[H]is fellow classmates talked about taking Roy's discards and holding onto them, because they recognized that here was a guy in their midst who really knew what he was doing while most of them said, "You know, we were trying to understand, and here was Roy throwing away stuff that we would have loved to have done." [12]

In 1950, Lichtenstein was denied tenure at Ohio State. His teaching contract was not renewed for the 1951-52 academic year, and in the autumn of 1951 he and Isabel moved to Cleveland, where the couple had friends and she could find work. Isabel Lichtenstein became an interior decorator specializing in modern design, with a clientele drawn from wealthy Cleveland families. Whereas her career was on the rise, Roy did not continue to teach at the university level. He had a series of part-time jobs, including draftsman, furniture designer, window dresser and rendering mechanical dials for an electrical instrument company. In response to his commercial work, he introduced quirkily rendered motors, valves and other mechanical elements into the paintings and prints. In 1954, the Lichtensteins' first son, David, was born; two years later, their second child, Mitchell, followed. Joseph O'Sickey, Lichtenstein's closest friend in Cleveland, said that by about 1956:

He had a whole series of very nice mechanical things that were very amusing – a lot of meters, pointers and threads and thermometers. It's interesting that one of the drawing books he used was French's "Engineering Drawings", and in that book the illustrations were done by Hoyt Sherman. [13]

Sidney Chafetz: *His experience in Cleveland, where he taught at a commercial art school, may have influenced his interest in these kinds of things, where he had to teach students how to represent, exactly, a certain product. I hadn't thought about this relationship before, but perhaps that triggered it, initially. Because at Ohio State, he wasn't interested in that at all.* [14]

By the late 1950s, the Lichtensteins' marriage was strained. Isabel was running a successful business, but she was becoming progressively dependent on alcohol. Roy had never found employment commensurate with his professional experience or ambition, and at one point he was installing curtains for his wife's clients. Lee Csuri, a sculptor married to Chuck Csuri, said:

Cleveland was Isabel's territory. She had a lot of clients, and she was the money-maker … Roy was very despondent about what he was doing … And just feeling that he was nowhere. [The work] was sort of Abstract Expressionist, but it was very … muddy. [15]

Lichtenstein was losing his identity as an artist, and the situation may have threatened his masculine pride. To salvage his career, he accepted a position as an assistant professor at the State University of New York at Oswego, in the north-

Roy Lichtenstein working on *Untitled*,1960,
in his house in Highland Park, New Jersey
© Samuel G. Weiner

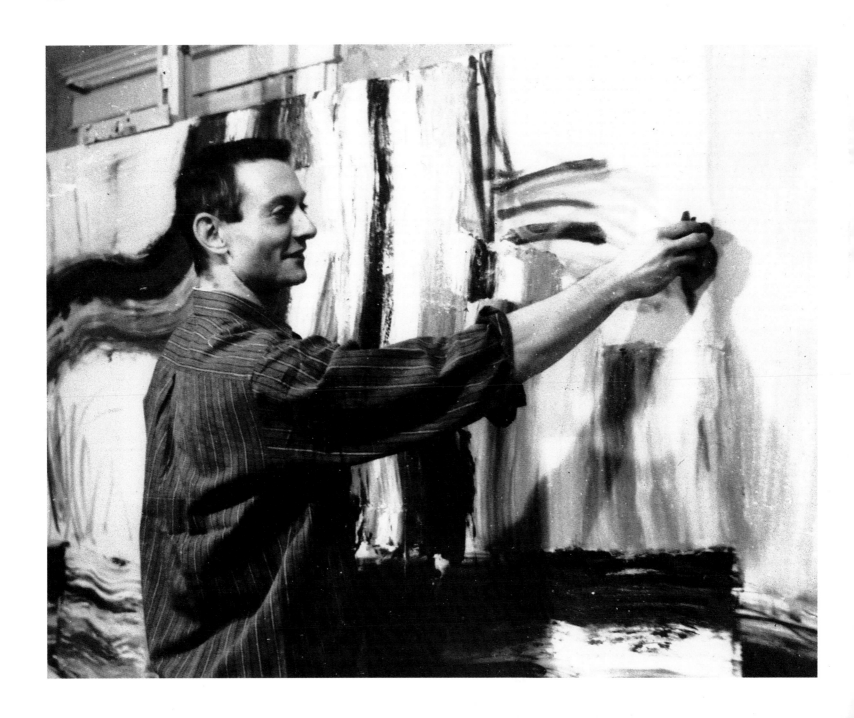

ern reaches of the state. Isabel did not leave Cleveland willingly, but she acquiesced, and Lichtenstein began teaching at Oswego in September 1957, along with three other new faculty members – David Campbell, Harvey Harris and Bruce Breland. Breland and his family shared a two-family house with the Lichtensteins when both men were first hired.

Most of the students taking the art courses were going to be industrial design teachers rather than artists.

Bruce Breland: *Roy was very popular with them. They liked him [b]ecause … he wasn't dealing with art as a mystery. He was dealing with art in the present, and they could understand that. "Here's how you make it."*

He didn't spend a lot of time speaking art history speak, he spent a lot of time with, "How does this go together? And how does it come apart?" He was constantly thinking up different ways of making different kinds of what he called "art marks". "Art marks" was a … [term] I heard a good bit of. That impressed me, because I'd never thought of the word[s] "art mark". And that comes directly from "Every mark you make modifies what you already know," [from] his old teacher.[16]

Lichtenstein introduced the flash room, the method Hoyt Sherman promulgated at Ohio State.

Bruce Breland: *He taught two-dimensional design, which turned into a flash room. He even had a machine that he converted to a kinesthescope, which is a strobe that flashes, and the shutter goes at a twentieth [of a second], or something like that. The idea behind that is that when you see something high-contrast, fast, … and it's very bright, there's a long after-image, and you draw the after-image. That was the whole thing – what's going on … in the head … We carry around images in our head, and we can draw from those … Every mark modifies what you already know. There's almost a catechism with it. I was taken with that. So Roy and I were just great conversationalists with each other. We tended to reinforce.*[17]

Living in Oswego was disastrous for the Lichtensteins. The winters were brutal and Isabel lacked fulfilling work. She became bored and hostile, and began drinking in earnest. As in Columbus and Cleveland, Roy was composing within the frame of reference that he would maintain throughout his working life, but he had not found a mode of expression that would transform his subject matter into an aesthetically vital concept. He painted a number of interiors – an idea to which he would later return so memorably – and made tentative drawings of Donald Duck and Mickey Mouse.

Roy Lichtenstein: *I had tried it [introducing comic book characters] quite a bit earlier. In 1958 I did some drawings with comic book characters. I had an idea about doing clichéd art.*

I thought of a table with curtains in the window and fruit on the table. All things I did later but it was different. I wasn't thinking of cartoons in 1958. I was thinking I could make it as dumb as possible.[18]

Bruce Breland: *What you had to understand was that his career was the most important thing for him, outside of his kids. [B]y the time he met Ivan Karp, he had shown in New*

York *– with no results. He was showing paintings, and they were going stone-nowhere.*[19]

In 1957 or 1958, Lichtenstein's mother and stepfather (his father died in 1946) visited the family in Oswego.

Bruce Breland: *His parents were visiting over the weekend, and this was the first time I ever saw him do this. Isabel was like, "Oh, oh." He got up in the middle of the meal. He goes upstairs to his studio, and he doesn't come down. He stayed there the rest of the weekend. That's the way he was. I really admired him for that. I was thinking, "Boy. I'm not driven by the same machinery he is."*

[He had] total focus. That's why I think it was in his nature to be that way, and I think that's why he never really said very much. He didn't react to people – he created a kind of distance.

I think he was hell-bent on getting recognized in New York … he understood that if he was going to realize his work, he was going to have to have it shown in New York. When he went to New York he had this big box, this old station wagon, filled with paintings. He'd go to New York, and every now and then I'd see that thing parked somewhere in New York, and I'd think, "Oh, Roy's in town."[20]

In the early winter of 1959, Lichtenstein, Breland and Harris went to the annual meeting of the College Art Association held that year in Washington, D.C.

Bruce Breland: *I decided I'd had it with the State University of New York and art programs that followed a state formula … About that time I met my old friend, Reggie Neal, at a college art meeting in Washington, and he said, "How would you like to come to Southern Illinois University with me?" Reggie Neal got to Southern Illinois as the new department head. I hadn't been there a month when Reggie announced he had an offer from the state university of New Jersey, in New Brunswick. Would I be interested in joining him there? I said, "I just got here! I moved my family here, Reggie. We're settled. We've got the house, and I like this place."*

So I said no. Then he asked me – he knew about two people I worked with in Oswego from what I had told him. One was Harvey Harris. Reggie asked me, "What do you think of Harvey?" "Well," I said, "he's a very good teacher. He's a product of Yale, and Joseph Albers's program, and that's the way he teaches. But I think you ought to hire Roy Lichtenstein. Roy Lichtenstein came out of Ohio State. He teaches young people about all this drawing-by-seeing theory that came out of his association with Hoyt Sherman in Ohio."[21]

In 1960 Reginald Neal became head of the art department at Douglass College, the women's college at Rutgers University. Douglass was committed to strengthening and expanding its studio art program. Because of Breland's recommendation, Neal invited Roy Lichtenstein to apply for a position as an assistant professor.

Geoffrey Hendricks: *Roy was looking for a job near New York. We had advertised for someone interested in design … We interviewed a group of people, and it had gotten down to Roy and one other person, who was a much more traditional*

Roy Lichtenstein working on *Image Duplicator*,
in his studio at 36 West 26th Street, New York, 1962
© John Loengard, Getty Images / Time Life Pictures

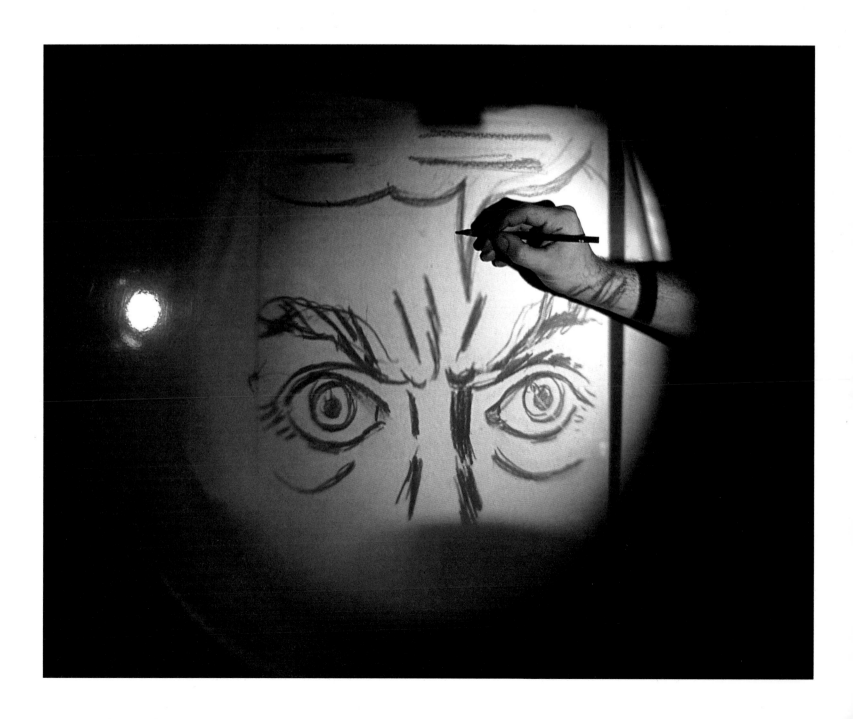

design person, who had come out of Yale and Albers colour theory and things like that.[22] Roy's background in design was through Ohio State, and he worked with a furniture designer – things like that. We were a bunch of artists, and we were interested in keeping a situation that was open and alive to art. Roy was very much more interesting to us as a person, so we decided on Roy.

He was teaching at Oswego, way up in northern New York, married, two kids. He arrived in this suburban van with a box on top that he'd built, that held these large striped paintings. He would put three or four colours onto plate glass, on the palette, saturate a rag with them, then draw it across and make a smear, and so forth. These were interesting. Here was an artist who was going ahead and doing big work and was obviously ambitious, but he also showed us slides – I don't know that he even had actual work – of paintings he'd been doing before, like "Washington Crossing the Delaware", "Custer's Last Stand", and these sort of playful, slightly cartoon-like images that related to American history. The striped paintings were the ones he'd done just before, and I guess our general feeling was that the cold of Oswego was making him too serious, or something. But, anyway, there was a connection there, so he got hired. He arrived the next day, and he got a house in Highland Park.[23]

Allan Kaprow: My recollection is that Reggie Neal, at that time, was the newly appointed chair of the art department at Douglass College … Then, along with a wonderful Dean – Mary Bunting – [he was trying] to staff his department … They all said, "Let's make this a real hot-shot department." Now who was there originally? Bob Watts was the key right there, because he was hired in the engineering school … He and I, and George Brecht and George Segal – those two lived there, but they were otherwise employed – a kind of quiet advisory group … they started hiring more people, with Mary Bunting's fiscal help. One of those calls, for somebody really international, came to me, on the other side of the campus. I guess they couldn't attract Rauschenberg or somebody like that to come and teach, but they had to continue their search. Their search turned up this character, whom I didn't know, called Roy Lichtenstein, from a New York university, way up in the north, called Oswego. Oswego had been in the news, because prior to that, the winter before, they had a huge snowstorm up there, and when Roy came for an interview – and none of us knew who he was – he pointed out, number one, that he shoveled his way out of his house. They had snow drifts of about six, seven feet high. So he managed to somehow shovel out a path, where the top of the snow was above his head. That endeared him, because his method of speaking about himself was very self-effacing, very kind of cool and withdrawn, at the same time humoristic. We liked him very much.

He told us … that he had been trained at Ohio State, before he went into the service, during the war, by a guy named Hoyt Sherman, [who had] invent[ed] a strobe light that made a flash, very, very quickly, that you could govern by a knob, so that it was either faster or slower. Roy said … he

didn't have a strobe light, … but he could invent one. He was very good at that sort of thing.

Eventually he bought a strobe light, but this intrigued everybody on the search committee – that he was going to train people to draw figures by a stroboscopic exposure to light, in a totally dark room. [The results were] fantastic … Somehow or other, in that very brief kind of assessment of vision, what each student learned was the overall image of a figure in motion, rather than a model on a stand – which was the old method … It was an introduction to abstract art, of course, because none of them, that I can recall, looked like people. They looked like marks, and they were quite wonderful.[24]

Teaching a course called "Art Structure," Lichtenstein once again imported Sherman's gospel, but during his first year at Douglass he was a less adventurous painter than his colleagues, particularly Watts and Kaprow. He continued with abstract paintings consisting of waves of pigment that resembled ribbon candy. The technique was ingenious and difficult to execute, said the painter Stanley Twardowicz, who saw Lichtenstein work on them in Highland Park, because "he picked up all the colours he had on the palette" and then transferred everything to the canvas in one movement.[25] He was experimenting with dragging paint, and the meaning of a brushstroke, which he would soon enough address in a Pop manner.

Letty Lou Eisenhauer was a graduate student in the art department who would collaborate with Kaprow, Claes Oldenburg, Dick Higgins and other avant-garde figures as a performer in their Happenings. When she first met Lichtenstein, Eisenhauer said:

Roy was painting small squares that gave the impression of mushy fields. The paintings were interesting, but Roy was very traditional at that point. He was really defending his turf – he had a clear idea about what was art and what was not art. For Bob [Watts], and Allan, and Rauschenberg, art and life were the same thing. There was no difference. But for Roy, art and life were separate things. That was the defense of the turf. Bob would take a stick off the ground and say, "Art," and Roy would say, "That's not art."[34]

Lichtenstein, although thrust into a maelstrom of artistic experiment, evinced little visible trepidation or anxiety. He emanated a quality that led the Rutgers group to believe in him very quickly.

Allan Kaprow: He was so cool, not only in his professional stance, but also in his family relations. There was a certain detachment that was present all the time. It might have led to some suppositions that, unlike the popular image of the tragic artist, Roy was just cool. He didn't have anything really exciting going on, the way artists are supposed to have exciting things going on all the time. I don't know, but my impression was that, after a very short time of having to ask myself, "What is this guy all about?" I began to really be sold on it. I was really quite convinced that whatever he was doing, it was very important. Subsequently, of course, he became the chef d'école, he and Andy.
[He had] an intangible quality, of high intellection but personal disavowal.[26]

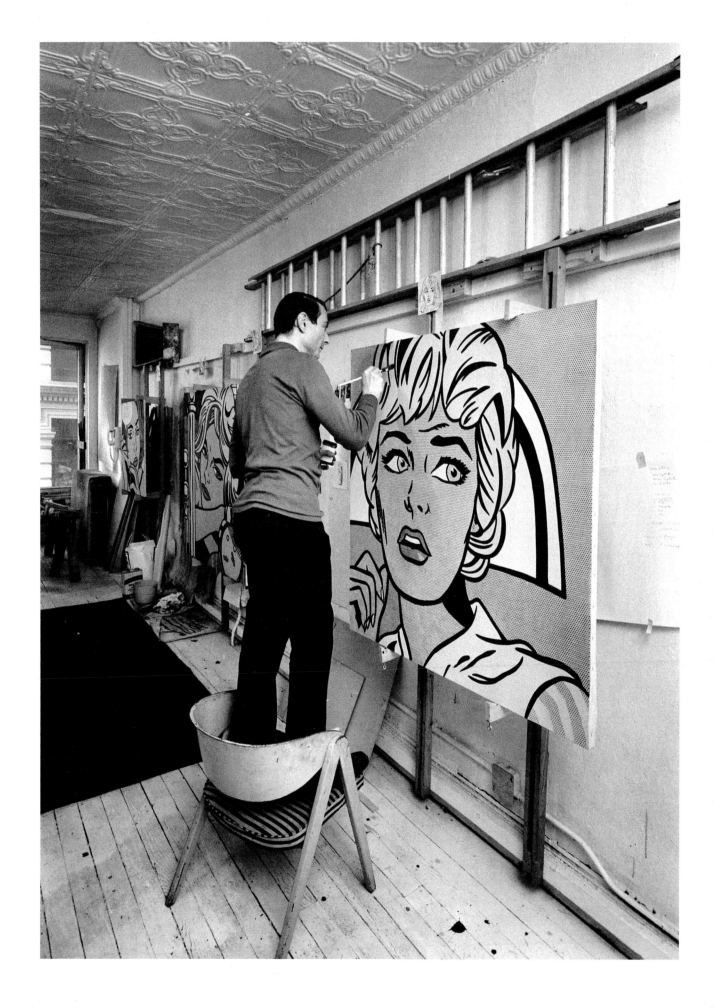

Indeed, Kaprow believed in Lichtenstein enough to help him try for more prestigious gallery representation, regardless of what he judged to be a flaccidness in his work.

Allan Kaprow: *He had been painting what he thought was the serious stuff that would get him into a major gallery in New York – he already had a gallery of nondescript reputation … But he and I could see that that was going nowhere, so I invited several gallerists … including … Martha Jackson. Martha Jackson … was in Europe, so I couldn't get her to come out and see Roy's paintings – which were then big, squiggly compositions of banded little clusters, which reminded me, in some regards, of Léger's early work. But it was done with real thick paint, the technique at that time that was favoured. I invited Steve Joy, who was one of the two gallerists that Martha had appointed during her absence in Europe. He came, and it was a dud. The visit was polite and nice, but it went nowhere. After a while, Steve said, "It won't fly."*[27]

Lichtenstein stated that in 1960, on his own, he brought this work to Leo Castelli, to no avail.

In January 1961, Lichtenstein exhibited twelve of the abstract canvases at Douglass College. He tried to secure a better gallery again at the end of March, when he brought his latest paintings to the sculptor Tom Doyle, a former student of his at Ohio State, who was living in downtown Manhattan.

Tom Doyle: *Roy was doing these striped pictures. He'd take a rag, load it, then drag it across the canvas. I was living at 431 Broome Street, and there was an empty floor. Roy asked if he could put his paintings up on this floor, and get [Henry] Geldzahler [the curator in charge of contemporary art at the Metropolitan Museum of Art] and Ivan Karp to come down and see them. I said, "Sure." So he brought them, and we put them up. They were supposed to come the next day. And I forgot. I was hungover and a buddy of mine from Ohio was in town. We went out, and when we got back there were cards in the door from them – because there was no one else in the building to let them in. Roy was not pleased. He didn't say anything, but the way it turned out, it's just as well, right?*[28]

Isabel Lichtenstein may have found Highland Park more congenial than Oswego, but her own situation was desperate. She was drinking from the morning until night, and often unable to take care of the children. Vaughan Rachel, who was married to Allan Kaprow while he was in the Rutgers faculty, observed:

Isabel had an office that was overflowing with bolts of cloth, plans, a telephone, and it looked like a very active workplace. She was quite unusual, as a working mother. I don't think, in actuality, she was doing that much commercial work at the time, but this was her office that she had brought with her from Ohio. There was a lot of tension in the family, between Roy and Isabel … Isabel, I think, was having a difficult time fitting into this new environment that included New York City, Roy's ambition at that point, and the attention that began to be paid to him … She would get loud and angry, just in general, and make sarcastic comments.

I think it was very hard for her to accept almost a role reversal. I don't remember talking to her about it, but I do know I couldn't understand this wonderful office upstairs, with all these bolts of fabric, the telephones, the books, all this evidence of a life that had been. Where was it now? So she probably felt deprived.[29]

Sandra Soll, then Sandra Levowitz, met the Lichtensteins in 1960 when they moved to Highland Park. An art student at Douglass, she was 21 years old, lived nearby, and became their friend. In June 1961, between her junior and senior years at Douglass, Soll began a Yale-Norfolk fellowship in art for the summer. When she left, she recalled that Lichtenstein was still working on "impastoed, striped paintings with the squiggles and the raw canvas."[30] From the accounts of witnesses, it seems clear that *Look Mickey* [1961; National Gallery of Art, Washington, D.C.], Lichtenstein's first surviving Pop painting, was executed in mid- to late June of 1961, but it was not as untoward a development as people who saw it surmised.

Roy Lichtenstein: *I was … immersed in Abstract Expressionism – it was a kind of Abstract Expressionism within the expressionist image. It's too hard to picture, I think, and the paintings themselves weren't very successful. I've got rid of most of them, in fact all of them. They encompassed about six months. I did abstract paintings of sort of striped brush strokes and within these in a kind of scribbly way were images of Donald Duck and Mickey Mouse and Bugs Bunny.*[31]

Indeed, Joseph O'Sickey recalled seeing charcoal drawings of Mickey Mouse and Donald Duck in the late 1950s, and Eleanor Madonik, a student of Lichtenstein's from Ohio State, remembered a visit to the Lichtensteins that occurred in 1957. She saw a painting with an image of Donald Duck.

Eleanor Madonik: *I remember the Donald Duck painting … on an easel. I saw the original [for "Look Mickey"] … But, instead of having it cropped in around the figures – [the way "Look Mickey" is] – … the figures are right here in the middle. Mickey Mouse was there, Donald was there. Donald was much more Disney-ish. This is really a caricature of the Disney duck. Donald, though, didn't look like this. The face wasn't bent up like that – which I think is marvelous. The exaggeration is what it needs. The tail was filled in, the square was there for the plank, the pier that they're standing was there. The pier was there, but it was more yellow. Everything was yellow. This background … was yellow. There was a line there, a horizon line, but there was more yellow. The whole thing had a huge amount of yellow around the figures, and just a little bit of a sense of water down here. It wasn't this kind of water. It was just blue, I think, with maybe a break or two. But I remember this yellow. [With "Look Mickey",] he brought it in, tightened it up, and made a real composition out of it, and exaggerated things that needed to be exaggerated.*

There was too much yellow background around them, and they needed to be composed. You needed to put a frame around them, and figure out where the point was to cut off some of that yellow background. And he certainly did, in the finished work.[32]

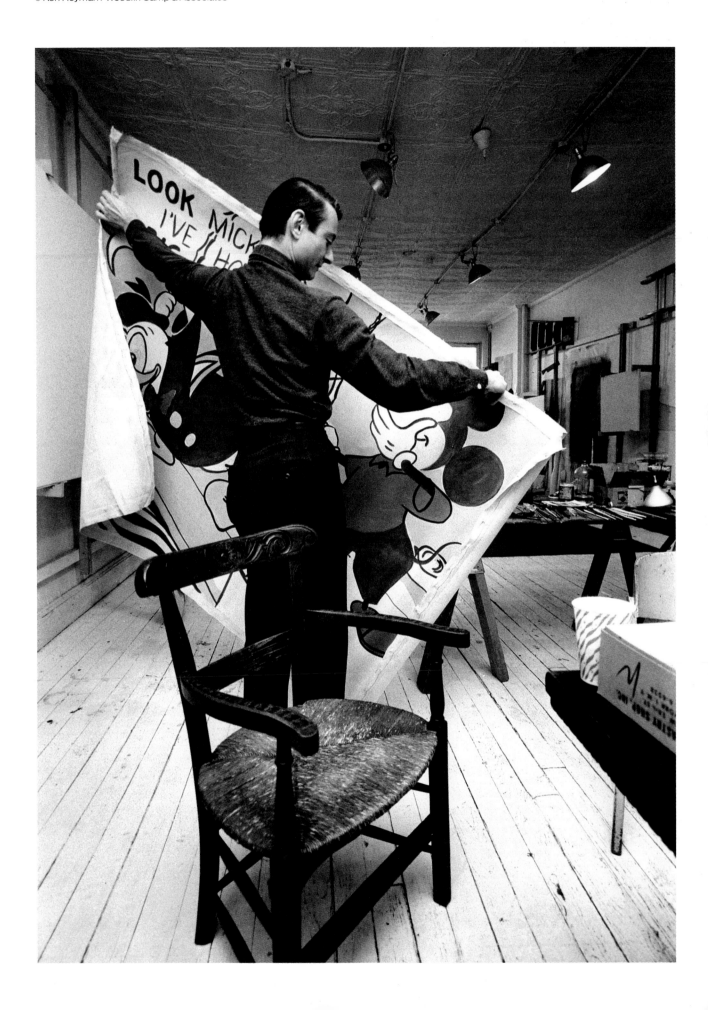

Roy Lichtenstein: *There's a sense of order [in comic strips] that is lacking. There is a kind of order in the cartoons, there's a sort of composition, but it's a kind of a learned composition. It's a composition more to make it clear, to make it read and communicate, rather than a composition for the sake of unifying the elements. In other words, the normal aesthetic sensibility is usually lacking, and I think many people would think it was also lacking in my work. But this is a quality, of course, that I want to get into it.*[33]

On June 24, 1961, Geoffrey Hendricks got married. Isabel did not attend the ceremony, so Roy went to the wedding with Letty Lou Eisenhauer.

Letty Lou Eisenhauer: *Roy and I were in his old station wagon. All I was interested in was getting beer, and all he was interested in was telling me about these paintings.*

He said, "I want to tell you about this painting I just did," and it was the Mickey Mouse one. I remember we were right in back of the bus terminal, we were in the car, and I'm saying, "Yeah, yeah. Turn here. We've got to stop over there, because I have to get this beer for the party afterward." I think everybody was coming, after the reception, to my loft downtown … He must have painted that painting then, right around that time.[34]

Roy Lichtenstein: *The idea of doing … [a cartoon painting] without apparent alteration just occurred to me. … and I did one really almost half seriously to get an idea of what it might look like. And as I was painting this painting I kind of got interested in organizing it as a painting and brought it to some kind of conclusion as an aesthetic statement, which I hadn't really intended to do to begin with. And then I really went back to my other way of painting, which was pretty abstract. Or tried to. But I had this cartoon painting in my studio, and it was a little too formidable. I couldn't keep my eyes off it, and it sort of prevented me from painting any other way, and then I decided this stuff was really serious. I had sort of decided that as I was working on it, but at first the change was a little bit too strong for me. Having been more or less schooled as an Abstract Expressionist, it was quite difficult psychologically to do anything else.*[35]

And then it occurred to me to do it by mimicking the cartoon without the paint texture, calligraphic line, modulation – all the things involved in expressionism.

I would say I had it on my easel for a week. I would just want to see what it looked like. I tried to make it a work of art. I wasn't trying just to copy. I realized that this was just so much more compelling.[36]

Allan Kaprow: *Roy's family and mine had children about the same time, and we began to see each other socially … One day [in June or July 1961] – it was a very hot New Jersey summer Sunday – we had a plan for the two families to have kind of a picnic lunch, or even a dinner. I don't remember exactly. But the families got together, and it became hotter, and more and more humid, during the afternoon. The two mothers decided to take the kids … to go get ice cream and do some shopping for dinner. Well, they came back about an hour later. Meanwhile, Roy and I were sitting in his*

converted bedroom, which was a studio, talking about pedagogy. For example, how do you teach art from Cézanne? I said you don't. That was my opinion. I said, "What you do –" and the kids had just come back with a bag full of Double Bubble chewing gum. They always had little cartoons inside, wrapped around the bubble gum. I said, "This is the way you teach colour, and volume, and composition." … Roy sort of looked at me with a slight grin.

… He smiled at me when I brought out that cartoon, suggesting that the high discipline of pedagogy could use pop imagery reproductions at that kind of level, rather than Cézanne. I said, "Cézanne's much too complicated. You'll never really teach Cézanne. It's just ninety-nine percent intuitive. This collapsing of space, and several viewpoints at the same time, will go right over the heads of the students. This is the way to do it. Teach them how to make cartoons," and he smiled at me. A half smile. He even then was a very, very prolific artist, so he had lots and lots of canvases tacked to the wall that had been on stretchers and he didn't have any more room. So he used the stretchers again and again, the way many of us did in those days, and tacked the paintings, in great big stacks, on the wall, with nails. So he flipped through a couple of these things and up came Donald Duck. He made some kind of silly excuse to the effect that one of his two boys came back complaining that his teacher asked all the students to tell what their daddy did, and that his two sons – or one of his two sons, in that particular class, it could have been David – was upset because he had to say his father was an artist. All the other fathers did something interesting and defensible, whereas being an artist was embarrassing to the kid. He said he made this Donald Duck thing – the one, "Look Mickey – I caught a big one," something like that. He did that to prove to David or Mitchell that he could draw.

Roy said he did that – I think it was a completely rationalized answer – to prove to Mitchell or David that he could draw. And the only way he could prove to Mitchell was to do cartoons. That was real drawing, whereas those clusters of banded colour and great big, thick paint, didn't make any sense to the boys, or to other students.

So I sort of guessed that this was nonsense, that he really liked that because he had shown me early work, which was sort of like Rufino Tamayo, a little bit like cartoonized, Piccasoid images, that were basically humoristic.[37]

Chuck Csuri: *My memory is that David came home one day … [and t]here was a section in his class where kids had to talk about what their parents did, and David said, "Joey's father's a policeman, and Henry's father is this, and Virginia's does this, etc. And you're an artist, and you can't draw." "Oh, okay." So he got out a canvas, and he drew this. Roy told me it had to do with what was going on in the classroom, and David, or David's experience with his classmates, and Roy's responding to David's concern.*[38]

Roy Pearce, a member of the Ohio State English Department faculty, and his wife, Marie, a bacteriologist, were friends of the Lichtensteins in Columbus, and they bought

Roy Lichtenstein in front of *Mirror #1 (6' x 3')*
in his studio at 190 Bowery Street, New York, 1971
Also pictured (left to right) *Mirror # 8 (36" diameter)*
and Mirror *#12 (24" diameter)*
© Renate Ponsold

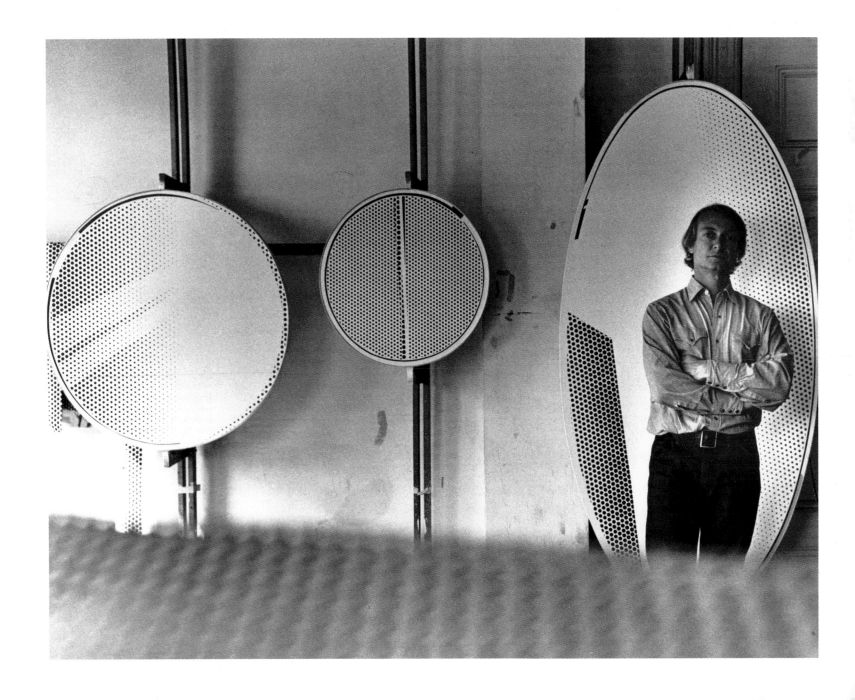

many of his early paintings. They stayed in touch, and in the summer of 1962, they visited Lichtenstein in New Jersey.

Marie Pearce: *The place was perfectly ordinary, and I think in one of the kids' rooms or somewhere there was a big Popeye. He didn't display his pictures, that I know of, around the house. They were usually stacked against the wall.*

Roy Pearce: *He didn't show me the Popeye until I asked him. I asked him about the origin of the Pop cartoon paintings, and he took me into the room and said he'd done this for one of his sons.*[39]

Allan Kaprow: *I was for a moment put off, but only for a moment, when I saw the cartoon. I thought, "This is it." So he and I sat there and plotted how he was going to get this into another gallery, so he could be noticed for cartoons. We momentarily discussed that he might have a show at the Judson Gallery, which I was temporarily in charge of. Then, after discussing this … I could see he really wasn't interested in showing in that avant-garde little gallery at the Judson Church. He really wanted the big time … I said to Roy at that point, "Let's go right to the top. Sidney Janis is the only other one that we could consider, and he's completely filled with a few stragglers from Abstract Expressionism. I don't think right now he could help, but I'll ask Ivan Karp."*[40]

Lichtenstein has stated that the picture Kaprow saw was *Look Mickey*, and it is his earliest extant Pop painting. However, the curator Diane Waldman, who organized Lichtenstein's two retrospectives at the Guggenheim Museum, reported that after his first discussion with Kaprow, Lichtenstein "destroyed those earliest paintings featuring cartoon images, and shortly thereafter … painted *Look Mickey*. It was, he recently remarked, his 'first painting with no Expressionism in it.'"[41] Vaughan Rachel confirmed seeing a precursor to *Look Mickey* with solely a Donald Duck figure in it. In the interview quoted above, Kaprow definitely recalled seeing Donald Duck and appended the title of "Look Mickey" to it as an afterthought.

Geoffrey Hendricks: *Well, he got into this, and began to make his first few paintings. He had questions, certainly, that were verbalized, verbalized to maybe all of us. He referenced a conversation he had with Allan Kaprow, who was saying, "Roy, try it and see where it goes. You can always go back to the striped paintings if it doesn't seem to make sense. But if you have a desire to do this, go do it."*[42]

Roy Lichtenstein: *The lines in "Look Mickey" now look rather rugged. And you can see the pencil marks all through it. The dots were put on by a plastic brush that I just dipped into the paint. It was kind of messy-looking. It was never exhibited and never offered for sale. In fact, nobody had seen it until much later. Leo at the time preferred paintings that were drawn more carefully.*[43]

Once Lichtenstein had made a breakthrough with a technique synonymous with his subject matter, he was eager to meet with Ivan Karp, who was assisting Leo Castelli, New York's leading dealer in contemporary art. Castelli had introduced Jasper Johns, Robert Rauschenberg and Frank Stella,

and his gallery, said Karp, was "the outpost for really threatening new things."[44] But the appointment would have to wait until the autumn because New York galleries were inactive in the summer. In the meantime, Lichtenstein had to prepare paintings for Karp's appraisal, and decisively severed himself from his former way of painting.

Roy Lichtenstein: *I started to do these [Pop paintings] seriously. I used all those other paintings – the abstract ones – as mats. I was painting in the bedroom and I put them on the floor so I wouldn't get paint on the floor. They got destroyed … I just walked on them and let paint drip on them from other paintings. Then I threw them away – about a dozen or so.*[45]

Geoffrey Hendricks: *I think once he made that decision, that things were going to shift, and that came through that summer, with that conversation with Allan and so forth – he was committed to trying it. This was his nature. He was organized and focused, and would lay things out.*[46]

In Harold Rosenberg's phrase, Lichtenstein's essential insight was squarely in "the tradition of the new." From Baudelaire to Duchamp to Jasper Johns, the potential of a vernacular or quotidian object to revitalize contemporary art by endowing it with a perceived authenticity has been a trope of modern art. Lichtenstein, who had long dealt with *outré* images, varied the conceit by aping a supposedly simple-minded style. Indeed, the very act of detaching that style from its original commercial context altered its fate. The perception of that style was transformed, rendering it unrecognizable *except as art*.

Allan Kaprow: *He would tell me that he was most interested in [Western] European clichés; that is, the kind of thing that becomes standard imagery … He said, "For example, the Benday dots are one of those things that signifies a half-tone. It's not in itself a half-tone, because the dot is a real dot. But it signifies that, and the nose of a standard American beauty queen is two vertical little commas, not the outline of the nose at all; and that a standard male, handsome male, is a single line for the top of the lower lip, then a shadow under the lower lip." He was fascinated by that. Those are cultural attributes that become, through over-usage, pure cliché.*[47]

After *Look Mickey* and *Popeye*, among the paintings that Lichtenstein completed for his appointment at Castelli were *The Engagement Ring*, *Girl with Ball* [Museum of Modern Art] and *Step-on-Can with Leg* [Kaiser Wilhelm Museum, Krefeld]. He also began a series of black-and-white paintings.

Allan Kaprow: *He told me, at some point, even perhaps very early, that all kinds of well-meaning friends give him images, and they are all wrong. He said, "I've never used any of these suggestions, even though they're well meant."*[48]

Roy Lichtenstein: *I chose [comic strips] that, when isolated, would say something. It was a question of both content and composition: the overall architecture, the dark and light composition, and maybe the absurdity when taken out of context. It is hard to say precisely what it was. Anyway, they were so simple-minded, so typical, that they had a provoking side. But I wasn't using only comic strips, sometimes*

126

Roy Lichtenstein working on *Figures in Landscape*
in his studio in Southampton, New York, 1978
Also pictured: Reclining Nude
Photographer unknown. Reproduced in OGGI, 1978
Courtesy Roy Lichtenstein Foundation Archives

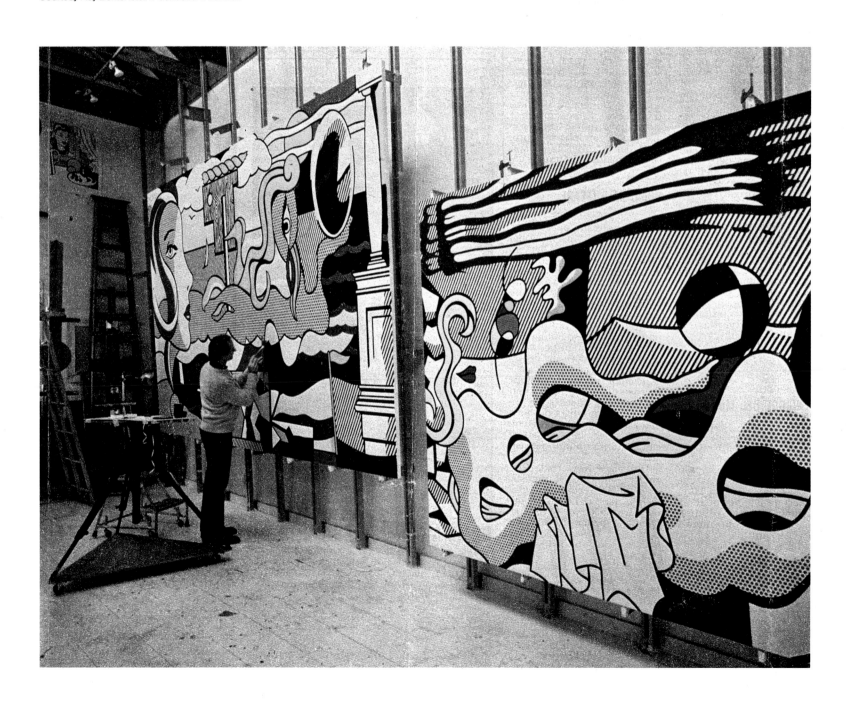

I picked ads of common objects. It would also interest me whenever an illustration looked like art, somebody else's art. For example, the "Tyres", whose pattern reminded me of Stella's work, and the "Composition Book", whose cover looked like a Pollock painting but also read "compositions" on its label. [49]

Vaughan Rachel: *I remember phone calls. I remember being at my new house. We were still unpacking boxes, and there was a phone call from Roy Lichtenstein. Roy was asking Allan to set up that appointment with Castelli. He wanted Allan to get on that for him … We probably moved, I'd say, July or August [1961], maybe … I do know there was a phone call, and I also knew – when Roy made that call to Allan, I was aware that this was something in process, that he was doing this. Whatever he was trying to set up had been started before.* [50]

In late August 1961, Sandra Soll returned to Highland Park from her fellowship at Yale:

I think the first place I went was to the Lichtensteins', because they were like a family to me. Isabel pulled me aside, literally, and said, "You are not going to believe what you see when you go upstairs." I couldn't imagine what she was talking about, [but] it was a shocking experience … [T]here were the Donald Duck paintings, the Mickey paintings, and there were all these stencils of dots. Roy used to paint them on one at a time, but then he got very swift about it, and he had all these different sizes of stencils cut.

It really was shocking, because he seemed to have such a passionate tie to Abstract Expressionism at its most abstract, or non-objective, and to come back and see these cartoon paintings – and they were huge. I just made the assumption that he was doing it for the kids, and he told me he was doing it for the kids … But then he brought out some more things, and they were of the same basic genre. They may not have been Donald Duck and Mickey Mouse characters, but they were definitely comic characters.

I just didn't know what to say at that point. It didn't make any sense to me. I didn't understand where it had come from, where he had come from. Isabel just thought the whole thing was absurd.

One of my professors at Yale was … Jon Schueler. He came to visit me for the weekend, and I said, "Would you like to go over to a friend of mine and see some paintings that are really radically different from anything I think you've ever seen, on large canvases?" Jon, who was pretty much an abstract classicist, said, "Sure." [W]hen we went upstairs and looked at the work, Jon said, "I know the perfect person for you to show this work to. You should show this work to Leo Castelli. He will love it."

… Jon said, "If you want me to call him, I'll tell him to come out here and take a look at what you're doing." I don't know if that had anything to do with Leo Castelli having this major interest in Roy's work, but Jon was certainly right on the mark. He had shown with Castelli in a different period, and he knew pretty much what Castelli was after in terms of new images, and radicalism … But he thought they were absolutely banal. [51]

During the academic year of 1961-62, Geoffrey Hendricks, who lived in Manhattan and commuted to Douglass, had a late evening class on Thursday and another one that followed on Friday morning. Beginning in September 1961, he stayed over at the Lichtensteins' house, sleeping in the spare bedroom that was used as a studio.

Geoffrey Hendricks: *I'd stay in his studio one night a week, on the cot that was there, then have breakfast, and drive back to school with Roy. So during that time period I was seeing the emergence of all these first paintings …*

"The Engagement Ring" was in our faculty show that fall. I remember, there, talking with – well, the shock and surprise of people in the administration, then other colleagues in other departments who were seeing it, and talking and defending it. The "Roto Broil" [1961] I saw when it was getting done. And very much, the "Girl with Ball" … [I saw it] on the easel, and the little ad that he had. Then the ball of string [Ball of Twine; 1963; Hessisches Landesmuseum, Darmstadt] – well, invisible reweaving ["Like New"; 1962]. I definitely remember Curtains [1962; St. Louis Art Museum], the "Black Flowers" [1961], definitely this "Bread in Bag" [1961; Städtisches Museum, Abteiberg].

Then there was a point [spring 1962] where Castelli wanted drawings, so he was doing what he was doing in the big things, in his drawings. He basically didn't make studies of them before. He would take the little image, like the clippings from advertising fliers, or comic books, and that would be what he would work with. And he would kind of draw with tracing paper, over them, maybe, then he would be drawing, or projecting, right onto the canvas, then masking out, then putting Benday dots. [52]

The predominance of black-and-white compositions occurred in autumn 1961, Hendricks said, "because they were like the newspaper illustrations."

Geoffrey Hendricks: *He reduced things down to three colours, or red, yellow, and blue got added to the black, because they were the ones that were the primary things that would come into printing, and that you'd have in comic strips. It was simple, basic things, but it was a long time before he came in with green. That [introducing another colour] was really pretty radical.*

He was feeling the constraints of the print process as a parameter, like writing a haiku or a sonnet or something. There are certain forms that you have to adhere to. So that cheap printing was black-and-white … And then, okay, you can bring in the primaries – red, yellow, blue – which you get in comic strips. But then to get into a green was crossing another boundary there, in a certain way.

[Benday dots were] what you had in a newspaper ad. It seems to me he would look through a magnifying glass and – he talked about wanting to get this quality. It really got a hold of him. He really wanted to get something that would be a signature, that would be like a supermarket logo that was totally anonymous. And when you go ahead and have him making a self-portrait that's just this square of Benday dots,

Roy Lichtenstein working on *Portrait II*
in his studio in Southampton, New York, July 1981
© Michael Abramson

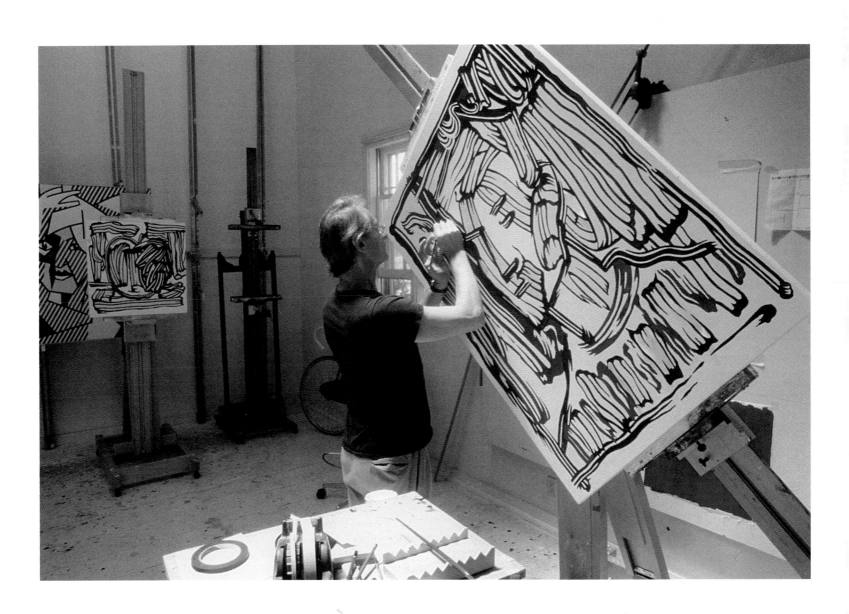

as a mirror, you see this kind of negating of self into the work that is implicit there, in the process of painting.[53]

Sandra Soll: *The idea of painting so many dots, in exactly the same line or row, just struck me as being funny. It was very mechanical, but he was totally absorbed. He would be like, maybe, a bird coming out of its shell, just affecting, and maybe even infecting, everything in his path in terms of his concentration … It was really an act of love. I think that's when he was feeling the most complete, and the happiest.*[54]

Ivan Karp: *Allan Kaprow … called me on the phone one afternoon and said there was a painter and teacher working out at Douglass College … who was doing some rather unsettling images. And Kaprow asked me if I would be so kind as to look at them. I said, "Well, you know, of course I'll look at him as I look at anybody's work … Does he have any slides?" "No, he had never taken any slides. Would you look at the paintings themselves because it's important to see them in person?" I said, "Yes, it's all right to bring them right to the gallery." Apparently the artist brought them in on top of his car … one afternoon when he wasn't teaching.*[55]

Roy Lichtenstein: *I went there [to the Leo Castelli Gallery, then at 4 East 77th Street] with the paintings on top of my station wagon, and as I was coming up the stairs, carrying a big picture, "The Engagement Ring", Ivan was talking to a class … He turned and without a pause said, "And this is the art of the sixties." So of course I felt wonderful. I put the painting and the others in the back room and spread them out. Ivan wanted to arrange things so Leo would like them. Leo came out and was very cordial. I think he needed to think about it a little bit. He asked me to leave them, which I was happy to do.*[56]

Allan Kaprow: *Roy had a beat-up old station wagon then, and at my suggestion he put a half-dozen paintings into the car and drove them to New York from Highland Park on a particular afternoon that I had made an appointment to see Ivan. We came into the gallery, lugging these painting behind us, and Ivan was there. Leo was in a meeting with Jack Tworkov and would be out in a little while, maybe half an hour or so. So Ivan and Roy and I planned an event for how to present Roy's work.*[57]

Ivan Karp: *I remember seeing Roy in the hall with them. They were all facing the wall. I said, "What are these?" He said, "Well, Mr. Kaprow called about me. I'm Lichtenstein and I wish you'd look at these paintings." There were five of them there. He turned them around in the hall, and it was a very jarring experience. I remember the first thing I said to him – "You really can't do this, you know." … It was just too shocking for words that somebody should celebrate the cartoon and commercial image like that. And they were cold and blank and bold and overwhelming. And I remember saying to myself, he can't do this, he just can't do this. I said it to him aloud. He said, "Well, I seem to be caught up in it. Here they are." … And I said, "Well, look, I'd like Castelli to see these. …" Roy and I put them in the back room. I made him take one back with him which I didn't like at all. It ["Look Mickey"] was just a little*

mushy cartoon picture. *But we kept, I think, four of them. And then Leo saw them and had his own set of reactions to them. Which was pretty startling. And we were both jolted.*[58]

Allan Kaprow: *I showed Ivan first. He never saw this before, and he was completely taken with it … Roy's surfaces were now completely clean, with a pronounced Benday dot that he used some screen to make. Ultimately, he would have manufactured a number of different sizes of Benday screens of metal, but at that point he did whatever he could … He said, "Oh, Leo's got to see this." So I said, "Can we make an appointment for next week?", and he said, "Don't. Let's do it right now." This was Ivan. He said, "Roy, you stay in the back, in the stacks, so when Leo opens the door, he'll see only one or two paintings." I said, "Let's show them all. Let's stack them here like cards, so that he and Jack Tworkov will have to confront them. Let's not make it an accident." "And Roy," I said, "you stand in the stacks and appear when you're called. All we want you to do is go, 'Gulp,' and we'll see what happens." We were quite convinced that this was going to be a dramatic confrontation.*

So sure enough, we got the paintings all stacked so that both Jack Tworkov and Leo couldn't possibly get out without seeing these paintings and wending their way through them. We stacked them at angles, so they would lead out to the outside door, from the stacks, and the stacks were just in front of Leo's office. Well, the door opens, Leo's in front, Jack is very close behind, and they stopped dead – I remember this – and Leo's eyes started going cross-eyed and his mouth did that kind of rubbery look that the cartoonists make when they want to show somebody who is discombobulated. He tried to smile. He couldn't. And right behind him Jack Tworkov, without guile or anything, started laughing very, very supportively. Not against the art work, but, rather, to show he really enjoyed it. And that was the beginning of Roy's success.[59]

Chuck Csuri: *Allan said, "Ivan Karp owes me a favour. Let's take them in to Ivan. Let's see what he thinks." Allan set up the appointment, they took the paintings into the Castelli Gallery, Ivan Karp looked at these things – "Hmmn. Kind of interesting" – but he didn't know quite what to make of them, either. "Why don't we show these to Leo?" Of course, that's what he wanted to do.*

Leo Castelli was in his office with Jack Tworkov having a conversation. So they put the paintings out in front of the office doorway, so that when Castelli came out, he would see them, and they would see what would happen. Tworkov came out first, saw them, and started laughing. He thought they were hysterical. I don't know what Castelli said but he was ambivalent, and Allan did his pitch about what these things meant. One thing led to another, and Leo said, "Well, why don't you leave them here for a while? Let me think about them. Okay?" He kept them for … [a] period of time. It may have been a couple weeks, maybe longer … [T]hen Roy said Leo Castelli called him in one day, and told him he was going to make him world-famous. Just like that. Now that's what Roy told me.[60]

130

Roy Lichtenstein in 1986, with cheese doors, designed
for his 105 East 29th Street, NYC studio elevator
© Bob Adelman

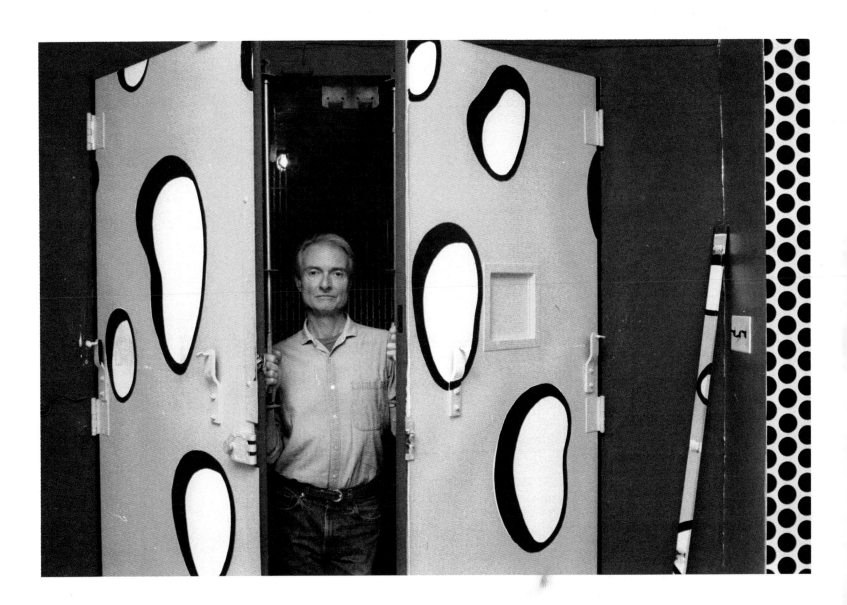

Ivan Karp: *We thought … we'll put them in the racks and we'll take them out again and see how they feel as the days go by … we showed them to people who came into the gallery. And it was not good … There were really truly unpleasant moments … because people thought that if we'd show art like that, it would be the end of our situation.*[61]

Sidney Chafetz: *[In September-October 1961] I went with him one time to Castelli's, when Castelli was considering Roy. So we went in, Ivan Karp was there, and Roy was saying, "Look, I can't sleep at night. Which way is Leo going to decide?" And Karp said, "Roy, relax. Leo's going to choose you." Roy said, "I hope so."*[62]

Letty Lou Eisenhauer: *I was there when the first Pop paintings were sold. I was going out with Billy Klüver at the time, and we were good friends with Ileana Sonnabend [formerly Ileana Castelli, Leo's first wife. She opened her own gallery in 1962]. She came to us and said, "I saw these paintings in the gallery, and I'd like to meet the artist, but don't tell Leo." So we went. We took her to Roy's house in Highland Park. He showed her all these paintings, and that day she bought either two or three – small [ones], about 18" x 24" and Billy bought "Transistor Radio". When we were getting ready to leave, Roy said to me – he was holding these checks in his hands – "If I take these to the bank, I'll get real money?" Although he had sold paintings before, I think he was stunned to sell three paintings to a dealer who was greatly respected for her eye. I think she paid … maybe $300 a painting. When we left, Ileana said, "Don't tell Leo that I bought these paintings, for a couple of days." It was discussed widely that was Ileana who made many of the creative, artistic decisions, even in those days, for Leo … I think that's what created the situation of Leo finally taking Roy…*[63]

In October 1961, Castelli agreed to represent Roy Lichtenstein and pay him a stipend of $400 a month. *Girl with Ball* was sold to the architect Philip Johnson. Collectors Burton and Emily Tremaine and Richard Brown Baker subsequently purchased paintings. About this time, Roy and Isabel temporarily separated; Isabel had discovered that Roy was seeing another woman – a photographer who lived in New York City.

Ivan Karp: *When Roy's work was first shown here, it was much despised by our own art community … by artists, critics, collectors, almost universally … [J]ust a handful of people besides Leo and myself … were very surprised by Roy's art and very fascinated by it. The first artist in New York that I know of to have any kind of responsiveness to Lichtenstein was Salvatore Scarpitta … And I remember [he] said, "Why don't you just give in to it? You really seem to be taken up with this thing. Put one up there in the front room." We finally did. And there was much fierce antagonism to the idea of even having that work in the gallery … the subject matter alone was so alien to art's preoccupation … commercial things, objects from the newspapers that were very blunt, very bland, very cold, very numb in a way … [A] curator of a local museum who was a very close friend of the gallery came and said that we had gone too far and he would not be*

interested in visiting the gallery if work of this type was going to be shown here.[64]

Sidney Chafetz: *I remember coming back to New Jersey with Roy after Castelli had chosen him, and he said, "You know, my dream has come true. I always dreamed that one day the Seven Santini Brothers would march into my studio in their white coveralls and gloves, take the painting off the easel, bring it to New York, and gone would be the days when I had to strap the stuff to the top of my station wagon and shlep it to New York. It's a dream that came true. I can't believe it." By that time, he'd bought himself a sports car.*[65]

Allan Kaprow: *Leo and Ivan and Roy planned to mount a show very, very quickly and sell whatever they could, so they could put red dots all over the place, for peanuts. So all you had to do was just make sure you placed these paintings in the collections of famous people, and that would make a reputation. That had happened already with Jasper Johns, so I knew a little bit about the strategy and tactic.*

… The idea was, basically, have a big show, turn it over three times, or four times if you can; have Roy, who was working like a crazy fool, produce more cartoon paintings. It was really quite successful and it created a hubbub instantly, because you were dealing with the top people, in reputation anyway, at that early time when it seemed that Abstract Expressionism had played itself out, to many of the younger artists.

It was a perfect opportunity to introduce some new energy, and the time was just right … Roy handled it very well … He learned to be self-effacing as a style. Instead of the heroism of the previous generation's art, where you were macho, now the stance of the Pop artist, especially with Roy and Andy, was a kind of "gulp" stance. "Who, me?" … That's metaphorical, but essentially that was the way Roy positively advanced himself, without histrionics.[66]

From February 10 to March 3, 1962, Roy Lichtenstein had his first one-person exhibition with Castelli, and the reality of his success outstripped any fantasy he could have entertained. A year later, he took a leave of absence from teaching, permanently separated from his wife, and moved into New York City. In June 1964, Lichtenstein left Douglass College for good; soon after, he met Dorothy Herzka, whom he married in 1968. He persevered without distraction, producing paintings, drawings, prints, sculpture, and murals, becoming, in accordance with his temperament, said Allan Kaprow, "a very historical, intellectual artist of great, conservative humor."[67]

Fittingly, this ultimate connoisseur of clichés remained skeptical of the nature of sudden celebrity, the phenomenon for which he was so resented.

Bruce Breland: *He told me a story [about being in Europe after World War II ended] that was real interesting – going to Paris and standing in front of the studio door of Picasso but he didn't knock, and he didn't go up to see him. He hesitated. I always thought that was amusing, especially when Roy told it. He always had a way – there was a little bit of self-deprecation there. When I was talking to Roy, right after he started*

132

really showing his work in New York with Castelli, we were walking down the street together and he said, "You know, it's hard to believe, but I wonder how long it's going to last."[68]

Dorothy Lichtenstein: He joked [until] … the early '80s [about his success]. [H]e would say, "I know any minute someone's going to come and shake me and say, 'Mr. Lichtenstein, Mr. Lichtenstein, it's time for your pills,' and I'll be back in Oswego, in a wheelchair." [It was] fifteen or even close to twenty years into this success and working, … [before] he began to believe all the articles and the PR.[69]

Tom Doyle: [After] my first one-man show … there was a big party, and Roy came … It was a very wild affair – I got in a fight with this guy. We were going to go downstairs to finish this fight. We got in this little elevator and I said, "This is really stupid. Let's go back upstairs and forget about it," because it was over a woman … I remember coming out and saying, "Is it worth it? Is it worth it?" Roy said, "It's all worth it. It's all worth it." And he took me home.[70]

Avis Berman directs the oral history programme of the Roy Lichtenstein Foundation. She is the author of Rebels on Eighth Street: Juliana Force and the Whitney Museum of American Art (Atheneum, 1990) and James McNeill Whistler (Abrams, 1993) and editor of The Artist's Voice: Talks with Seventeen Modern Artists by Katharine Kuh (Da Capo, 2000). She has worked as an oral historian for the Metropolitan Museum of Art, the Museum of Modern Art, the Andy Warhol Museum and the Mark Rothko Foundation.

Acknowledgments and notes

All authors are indebted to their sources, but none more so than one who undertakes shaping a compilation of this nature and scope. I am deeply grateful to the 40 people who have so generously shared their memories with me, and I hope that they will not be disappointed in the use to which their words have been put. I am pleased to thank the staff of the Roy Lichtenstein Foundation – Jack Cowart, Cassandra Lozano, Clare Bell and Sarah Kornbluth – who have aided me so greatly with the advice, research and support that oral histories demand. In particular, Dorothy Lichtenstein has been unstinting in her encouragement, no matter where the inquiries might lead. I am equally happy to acknowledge the contribution of Valerie Davison, who transcribed every one of the interviews I conducted with patience and understanding. Only she knows how much I owe her.
Unless otherwise stated, the quoted material in this essay is drawn from the author's taped interviews conducted for the Roy Lichtenstein Foundation between 2001 and 2003, as part of the foundation's ongoing oral history project. The recordings have been transcribed, edited, corrected, and deposited in the foundation's archive for final processing.

1   Interview with Sidney Chafetz, May 22, 2002
2   Interview with Alvin Katz, July 2, 2002
3   Interview with Joseph and Algesa O'Sickey, March 4-5, 2002
4   Interview with Dorothy Lichtenstein, November 24, 2001, and July 5, 2002
5   Interview with Chafetz
6   Interview with Letty Lou Eisenhauer, February 27, March 20, and April 3, 2003
7   Ivan Karp, interview with Paul Cummings, March 12, 1969, Archives of American Art, Smithsonian Institution
8   Roy Lichtenstein, quoted in Milton Esterow, "How Could You Be Much Luckier Than I Am?," in Roy Lichtenstein: Interiors: Collages, Vienna, Galerie Ulysses, 1992, p. 12. This article, an interview with the artist, was originally published in the May 1991 issue of ARTnews
9   See the pioneering catalogue Off-Limits: Rutgers University and the Avant-Garde, 1957-1963, edited by Joan Marter, The Newark Museum, 1999, for a thorough survey of the Rutgers group's achievements
10   Interview with Chuck and Lee Csuri, May 24, 2002
11   Roy Lichtenstein, interview with David Sylvester, January 1966, quoted in Some Kind of Reality: Roy Lichtenstein inerviewed by David Sylvester in 1966 and 1997, Anthony d'Offay, London 1997, p. 7
12   Interview with Chafetz
13   Interview with Joseph and Algesa O'Sickey. The book to which Joseph O'Sickey refers is A Manual of Engineering Drawings for Students and Draftsmen, by Thomas E. French. It was originally published by McGraw-Hill in 1911, and remained in print through the 1970s. Updated editions that would have been available to Lichtenstein were printed in 1941, 1947, and 1953
14   Interview with Chafetz
15   Interview with Chuck and Lee Csuri
16   Interview with Bruce Breland, July 30-31, 2002
17   Ibid
18   Roy Lichtenstein, interview with Milton Esterow, p. 11
19   Interview with Breland
20   Ibid
21   Ibid
22   The other candidate may well have been Harvey Harris
23   Interview with Geoffrey Hendricks, April 19 and October 10, 2002
24   Interview with Allan Kaprow, August 24, 2001
25   Interview with Stanley Twardowicz, January 14, 2002
26   Interview with Kaprow
27   Ibid
28   Interview with Tom Doyle, January 21, 2002
29   Interview with Vaughan Rachel, October 6, 2001
30   Interview with Sandra Soll, November 2, 2002
31   Roy Lichtenstein, interview with David Sylvester, pp. 7-8
32   Interview with Eleanor Madonik, December 11, 2001
33   Roy Lichtenstein, interview with David Sylvester, p. 9
34   Interview with Eisenhauer
35   Roy Lichtenstein, interview with David Sylvester, p. 8
36   Roy Lichtenstein, interview with Milton Esterow, p. 13
37   Interview with Kaprow
38   Interview with Chuck and Lee Csuri
39   Interview with Roy and Marie Pearce, August 21, 2001
40   Interview with Kaprow
41   Diane Waldman, Roy Lichtenstein, Solomon R. Guggenheim Museum, New York, 1993, p. 21
42   Interview with Hendricks
43   Roy Lichtenstein, interview with Milton Esterow, p. 12
44   Ivan Karp, interview with Paul Cummning
45   Roy Lichtenstein, interview with Milton Esterow, p. 13
46   Interview with Hendricks
47   Interview with Kaprow
48   Ibid
49   Roy Lichtenstein, quoted in Ann Hindry, "A Conversation with Roy Lichtenstein," in Artstudio, Vol. 20 (Spring 1991), p. 8
50   Interview with Rachel
51   Interview with Soll
52   Interview with Hendricks
53   Ibid
54   Interview with Soll
55   Ivan Karp, interview with Paul Cummings
56   Roy Lichtenstein, interview with Milton Esterow, p. 12
57   Interview with Kaprow
58   Ivan Karp, interview with Paul Cummings
59   Interview with Kaprow
60   Interview with Chuck and Lee Csuri
61   Ivan Karp, interview with Paul Cummings
62   Interview with Chafetz
63   Interview with Eisenhauer
64   Ivan Karp, interview with Paul Cummings
65   Interview with Chafetz
66   Interview with Kaprow
67   Ibid
68   Interview with Breland
69   Interview with Dorothy Lichtenstein
70   Interview with Doyle

Chronology

1923
Roy Fox Lichtenstein is born on 27th October in Manhattan, New York. His father, Milton, is a real estate broker, his mother Beatrice is a housewife. In 1926 his sister Renée is born.

1928-36
While Lichtenstein is at kindergarten and grade school he takes an interest in science and drawing. In his leisure time he builds model planes and listens to the radio series *Flash Gordon*.

1936-40
Graduates from Franklin School For Boys in Manhattan. On Saturdays he takes lessons in watercolour painting.

1940
Attends a summer course at the Art Students' League taught by Reginald Marsh in anatomical drawing and Renaissance techniques, which Lichtenstein applies to big city subjects – boxing matches, the Coney Island fairground, Harlem jazz clubs. He then begins studying art with Professor Hoyt Sherman and others at Ohio State University.

1942
Begins to produce paintings inspired by works by Picasso and Braque.

1943-45
Military service takes Lichtenstein to England, Belgium, Germany and France. Along the way, he makes sketches of landscapes, soldiers and local people.
From October to November 1945 he studies history and French at the Cité Universitaire in Paris, but has to return to the USA when his father becomes seriously ill.

1946
Milton Lichtenstein dies. Lichtenstein is discharged from the US Army and awarded a medal for Meritorious Service.
Lichtenstein resumes his art studies at Ohio State University, where he also teaches younger students. He paints semi-abstract works inspired by the geometric forms of Cubism.

1949
Receives a Master's degree in Fine Arts and works as an instructor at Ohio State University until 1951.
Participates in his first group exhibition at the Chinese Gallery in New York. Marries Isabel Wilson, co-director of Ten-Thirty Gallery in Cleveland. The couple settles down in Columbus, Ohio. They will have two sons, David Hoyt (1954) and Mitchell Wilson (1956). At the end of the year he exhibits at Ten-Thirty Gallery, selling a few works.

1951
Loses his teaching job at the university. Moves to Cleveland, Ohio and for the next few years. Has a number of short-lived jobs as, among other things, a window dresser, draughtsman, model-builder and designer for the steel industry.
Works with 'Americana' subjects from the Wild West in the Cubist idiom.
Participates in the Brooklyn Museum's adjudicated exhibition. His woodcut *To Battle* wins him a Purchase Award, and ensures him a place in the museum's collection. The adjudicating committee includes Josef Albers.
Shows his work to New York galleries; the Carlebach Gallery in Manhattan presents his first one-man show with paintings and assemblages made of wood, metal and found objects.

1952
Participates in exhibitions at, among other venues, the Denver Art Museum, the Metropolitan Museum of Modern Art and the Pennsylvania Academy of the Fine Arts. Lichtenstein's art arouses wide attention – both positive and negative. The work *Knight Storming Castle* – a photo of a castle glued to a pencil drawing – is described by a critic as "like the doodling of a five-year-old".

1953
Begins to integrate material from printed advertisements in his paintings and compositions of wood.

1956
Makes a lithograph, *Ten Dollar Bill,* his first proto-Pop work Although the motif of the ten-dollar bill is broken up into Cubist fragments, the work heralds the emblematic use of popular consumer culture which makes its real impact at the beginning of the 1960s.

1958
Is hired as an instructor in art at the State University of New York in Oswego, where the family settles.
Starts to include references to cartoon figures like Bugs Bunny, Mickey Mouse and Donald Duck in his paintings, which also incorporate stylistic elements from Abstract Expressionism.

1960
Begins new job as Assistant Professor of Art at Douglass College, Rutgers University in New Jersey.
Allan Kaprow involved with Rutgers' Art Department, introduces Lichtenstein to Claes Oldenburg, Lucas Samaras and Robert Whitman. At the same time he makes the acquaintance of a number of artists who are later involved in the Fluxus movement – George Brecht, Geoffrey Hendricks, George Maciunas and others.

1961
For the first time, he projects pictures from a comic strip onto his painting *Look Mickey;* introduces the speech bubble and the printing technique of Benday dots into his paintings, and takes additional subjects from advertisements and the consumer industry. Joins the Leo Castelli Gallery, which sells several works to private collectors.

1962
Castelli presents the first one-man show of Lichtenstein's Pop art works.
Begins paintings based on war and romance comics, including a number of enlarged women's faces.

1963
Separation from Isabel (divorce follows in 1967).
Takes leave of absence from Douglass College and establishes a home and studio in Manhattan.
Hires an assistant.
The Guggenheim Museum presents the exhibition *Six Painters and the Object*, which besides Lichtenstein features Dine, Johns, Rauschenberg, Rosenquist and Warhol. The exhibition subsequently tours most of the USA.
In June the first European one-man show of Lichtenstein's works opens at the Sonnabend Gallery in Paris.

68.
Landscape studies. (1964)
Private Collection

69.
Untitled (Seascape With Clouds). (1964)
Private Collection

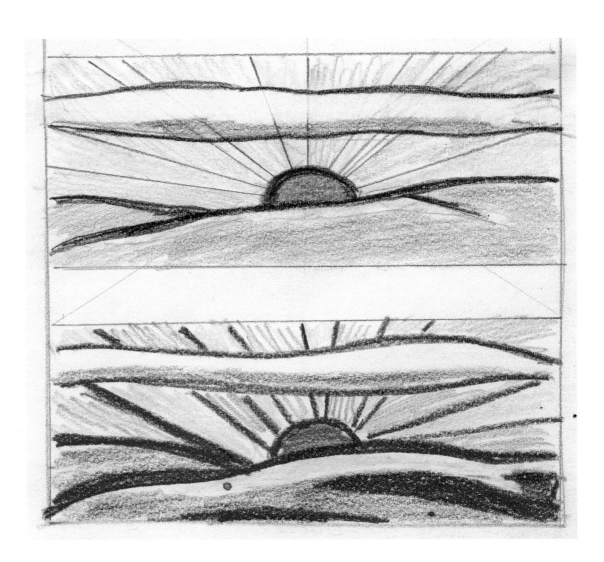

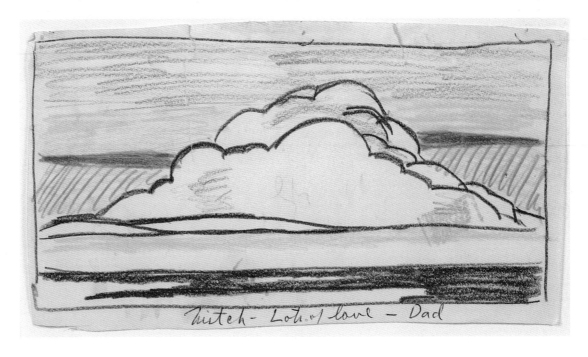

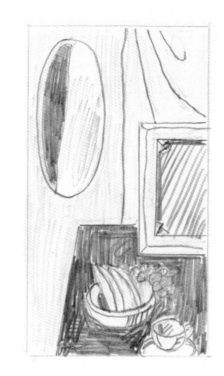

73.
Drawing for "Still Life with Mirror". 1972
Private Collection

74.
Drawing for "Artist's Studio 'Look Mickey'". 1973
Roy Lichtenstein Foundation Collection

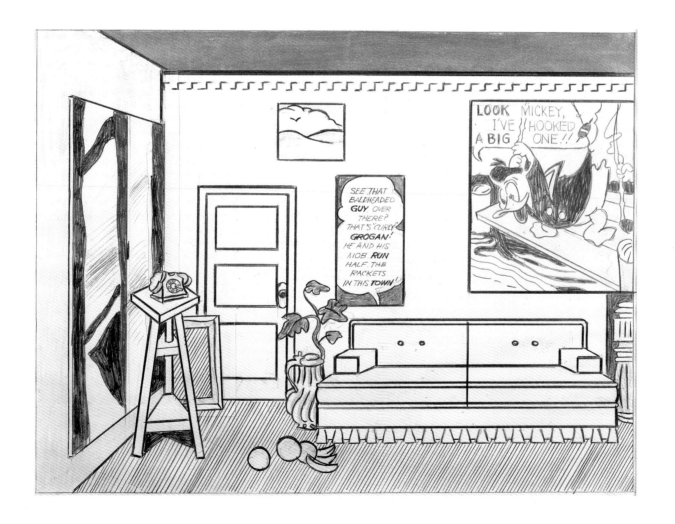

1964

Gives up his job at Douglass to concentrate on painting.

Life magazine features an article on Lichtenstein under the heading "Is He the Worst Artist in America?"

Does his first large-scale mural for the New York World's Fair.

Starts on a series of landscape paintings in a graphic style.

1965

Creates a group of enamel and steel sculptures based on explosions from comic strips, and makes a number of women's heads in collaboration with the ceramist Ka-Kwong Hui.

Starts on the series of *Brushstrokes* paintings.

1966

With Helen Frankenthaler, Jules Olitski and Ellsworth Kelly, represents the USA at the Venice Biennale.

The Tate Gallery in London purchases his large painting *Whaam!*

1967

Works with copper, mirrors, glass, aluminium and marble to make sculptures in the style of Art Deco.

Retrospective exhibitions at the Pasadena Art Museum in California and the Stedelijk Museum in Amsterdam.

1968-69

Marries Dorothy Herzka.

The Tate Gallery, London, presents a version of the Stedelijk's exhibition, the museum's first solo exhibition devoted to a living American artist.

First museum retrospective exhibition in New York at the Guggenheim Museum.

Modular paintings and serial images; series based on Monet's *Haystacks* and *The Cathedral in Rouen*.

Works on three films of sea views for the exhibition *Art and Technology* at the Los Angeles County Museum of Art, which opens in 1971.

1970

Two of the *Art and Technology* films are shown in the American Pavilion at Expo '70 in Osaka, Japan.

Moves to Southampton, Long Island.

1972-73

Paints a number of still lifes and the series *Artist's Studio* with references to Henri Matisse and to his own earlier works.

Diagonal stripes are added to his technical repertoire as another variant of half-tone.

1974-80

Works in idioms drawn from Surrealism, Italian Futurism and German Expressionism.

In 1979 he creates a commissioned sculpture, *Mermaid,* for the Miami Beach Theatre of the Performing Arts – a candy-striped mermaid in concrete, steel and enamel.

The same year he is inducted into the American Academy of Art and Sciences, and the next year is awarded an honorary doctorate at Southampton College, New York.

1981-82

Makes a series of four *Woman* paintings based on Willem de Kooning's series of the same name from the 1950s.

Works in an expressionist style, in which his earlier constructed brushstrokes are combined with looser, more 'natural' strokes.

The Saint Louis Art Museum arranges an exhibition of works from 1970-80, which tours the USA, Europe and Japan.

1984-87

Paints expressionistic landscapes and geometrical abstractions.

Paints *Mural with Blue Brushstroke* for the lobby of the Equitable Center, Manhattan.

Comprehensive traveling retrospective exhibition of Lichtenstein's drawings organized by the Museum of Modern Art, New York.

1988-90

Lives alternately in Southampton and Manhattan.

Creates the series *Reflections*, quoting Warhol and Picasso as well as his own early works.

Receives an honorary Doctorate of Humanities from Ohio State University.

Spends two months as artist-in-residence at the American Academy in Rome.

1991-92

With the series *Interiors* Lichtenstein returns to printed advertisements as his primary source of inspiration. These paintings are based on furniture advertisements and drawings from the Yellow Pages found in Italy and the USA. The exception is *Bedroom at Arles* – a paraphrase of Van Gogh's painting *Room at Arles* from 1888.

In the same period, he makes several sculptures including the 20-metre tall *Barcelona Head* created for the Olympic Games in Barcelona, 1992.

1993

The Guggenheim Museum arranges a retrospective exhibition which tours to Los Angeles, Montreal, Munich, Hamburg, Brussels and Ohio.

The Leo Castelli Gallery presents a new series of *Tintin* paintings based on the comic book character.

1994

Finishes a mural for the 42nd Street Subway Station, Times Square in New York..

1996

Works on a number of wood and bronze editions of *Brushstroke* sculptures.

The Leo Castelli Gallery exhibits the series *Chinese Landscapes*.

Donates 154 prints from his whole career to the National Gallery of Art to complement the Gemini G.E.L. archive, which contains examples of all the prints he produced at the printing house.

1997

The artist gives his last interview, to David Sylvester (reproduced in this publication) in New York.

New works, including his large-scale sculpture *House II* are presented at the Italian Pavilion of the Venice Biennale.

Roy Lichtenstein dies on 29th September as a result of complications caused by pneumonia.

List of works

*
Catalogue nos. 6, 11, 14, 22, 23, 24, 26 and 28 will be shown at the Louisiana Museum of Modern Art only

Catalogue nos. 18, 20, 20a and 30 will be shown at Hayward Gallery and Reina Sofía only

Catalogue no. 13 will be shown at Louisiana and Hayward Gallery only

PAINTINGS

1.
Bathroom. 1961
Oil on canvas
49 x 69 1/2 inches / 114 x 175 cm
Whitney Museum of American Art, New York
Gift of the American Contemporary Art Foundation Inc., Leonard A. Lauder, President, 2002.253

2.
Cup of Coffee. 1961
Oil on canvas
20 1/8 x 16 inches / 51 x 41 cm
Roy Lichtenstein Foundation Collection

3.
Look Mickey. 1961
Oil on canvas
48 x 69 inches / 122 x 175 cm
National Gallery of Art, Washington, DC;
Gift of the Artist and Dorothy Lichtenstein, in Honour of the 50th Anniversary of the National Gallery of Art 1990.41.1

4.
Popeye. 1961
Oil on canvas
42 1/4 x 56 inches / 107 x 142 cm
David Lichtenstein

5.
Radio. 1961
Oil on canvas with leather strap and aluminium stripping
17 1/4 x 20 inches / 44 x 51 cm
Private Collection, San Francisco

6.*
Roller Skates. 1961
Oil on canvas
42 x 40 inches / 107 x 102 cm
Private Collection

7.
Washing Machine. 1961
Oil on canvas
55 3/4 x 68 inches / 142 x 173 cm
Yale University Art Gallery, Gift of Richard Brown Baker, B.A. 1935

8.
ART. 1962
Oil on canvas
39 3/4 x 71 1/2 inches / 91 x 173 cm
Gordon Locksley and Dr. George T. Shea Collection, USA

9.
Desk Calendar. 1962
Oil on canvas
48 1/2 x 68 1/4 inches / 123 x 173 cm
The Museum of Contemporary Art, Los Angeles. The Panza Collection

10.
Golf Ball. 1962
Oil on canvas
32 x 32 inches / 81 x 81 cm
Private Collection

11.*
Masterpiece. 1962
Oil on canvas
54 x 54 inches / 137 x 137 cm
Collection Agnes Gund, New York

12.
Standing Rib. 1962
Oil on canvas
21 x 25 inches / 53 x 64 cm
The Museum of Contemporary Art, Los Angeles. The Panza Collection

13.*
Ball of Twine. 1963
Magna on canvas
40 x 36 inches / 102 x 91 cm
Courtesy The Brant Foundation, Greenwich, Connecticut

14.*
Cold Shoulder. 1963
Magna on canvas
68 x 48 inches / 173 x 122 cm
Collection Robert H. Halff

15.
Half Face with Collar. 1963
Oil and Magna on canvas
47 1/2 x 47 1/2 inches / 122 x 122 cm
Collection Gian Enzo Sperone, New York

16.
Image Duplicator. 1963
Magna on canvas
24 x 20 inches / 61 x 51 cm
Collection Charles Simonyi, Seattle

17.
In the Car. 1963
Oil and Magna on canvas
30 x 40 inches / 76 x 102 cm
Private Collection

18.*
Large Spool. 1963
Magna on canvas
68 x 56 inches / 173 x 142 cm
Sonnabend Collection

19.
Whaam! 1963
Magna on canvas
Two panels, 68 x 166 inches / 173 x 406 cm overall
Tate, London. Purchased 1966

20.*
Compositions II. 1964
Magna on canvas
56 x 48 inches / 143 x 122 cm
Sonnabend Collection

20a.*
Ohhh... Alright... 1964
Oil and Magna on canvas
36 x 38 inches / 91 x 97 cm
Collection Steve Martin

21.
Sussex. 1964
Oil and Magna on canvas
36 x 68 inches / 91 x 173 cm
Robert and Jane Rosenblum, New York

22.*
We Rose Up Slowly. 1964
Oil and Magna on canvas
68 x 92 inches / 174 x 235 cm overall
Museum für Moderne Kunst, Frankfurt am Main. Former Collection of Karl Ströher, Darmstadt

23.*
Big Painting VI. 1965
Oil and Magna on canvas
921/2 x 129 inches / 233 x 328 cm
Kunstsammlung Nordrhein-Westfalen, Düsseldorf

24.*
Brushstrokes. 1965
Oil and Magna on canvas
48 x 48 inches / 122 x 122 cm
Private Collection

25.
Landscape with Column. 1965
Oil and Magna on canvas
48 x 68 inches / 122 x 173 cm
Private Collection

75.
Drawing for "Fragmented Painting of Lemon and a Melon on a Table". 1973
Private Collection

76.
Drawing for "Still Life with Swiss Cheese". 1973
Private Collection

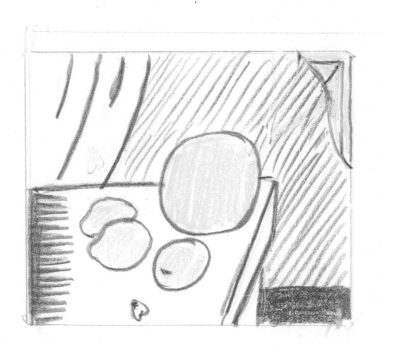

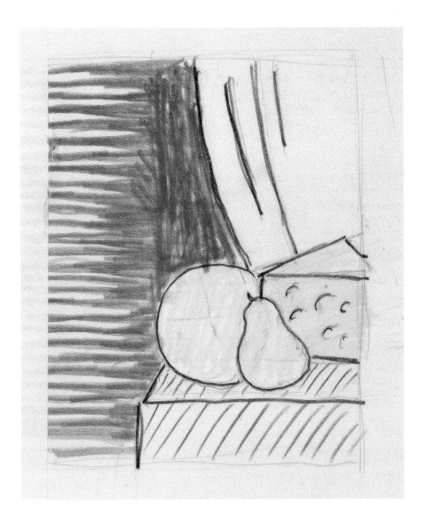

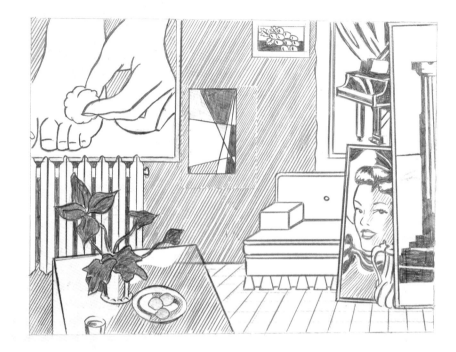

77.
Drawing for "Artist's Studio
'Foot Medication'". 1974
Private Collection

78.
Drawing for "Figures in
Landscape". 1977
Private Collection

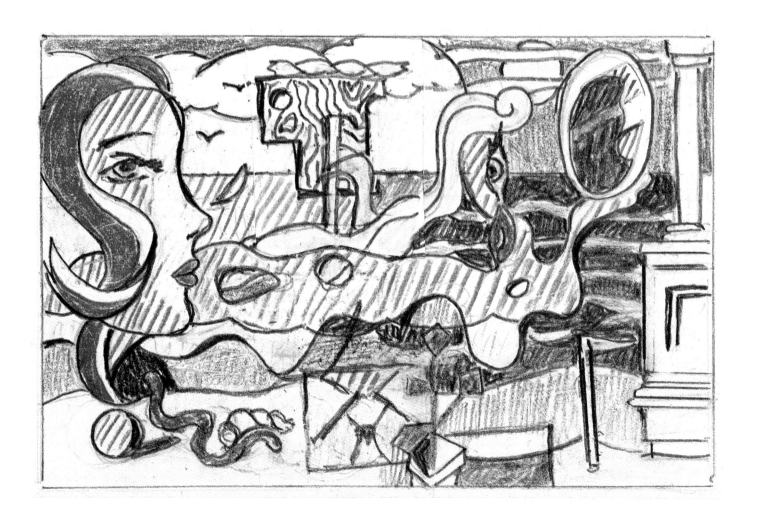

26.*
M-Maybe. 1965
Oil and Magna on canvas
60 x 60 inches / 152 x 152 cm
Museum Ludwig, Köln,
Ludwig Donation 1976

27.
Yellow Brushstroke I. 1965
Oil and Magna on canvas
68 1/8 x 55 7/8 inches / 173 x 142 cm
Kunsthaus Zürich

28.*
Yellow Sky. 1966
Magna on canvas
36 x 68 inches / 92 x 173 cm
Ulmer Museum, Stiftung Sammlung Kurt Fried

29.
Stretcher Frame with Cross Bars III. 1968
Oil and Magna on canvas
48 x 56 inches / 122 x 142 cm
Private Collection

30.*
Mirror #1 (oval 60" x 48"). 1969
Oil and Magna on canvas
60 x 48 inches / 152 x 122 cm
The Eli and Edythe L. Broad Collection

31.
Rouen Cathedral Set V. 1969
Oil and acrylic on canvas
3 panels, 63 1/8 x 42 inches / 160 x 107 cm
each // 63 1/8 x 126 1/4 inches /
160 x 320 cm overall
San Francisco Museum of Modern Art.
Gift of Harry W. and Mary Margaret Anderson

32.
Mirror in Six Panels. 1971
Oil and Magna on canvas
Each panel 120 x 22 inches / 305 x 55 cm
// 10 x 11 feet / 305 x 335 cm overall
Roy Lichtenstein Foundation Collection

33.
Still Life with Mirror. 1972
Oil and Magna on canvas
96 x 34 inches / 244 x 137 cm
Private Collection

34.
Still Life with Glass and Peeled Lemon. 1972
Oil and Magna on canvas
42 x 48 inches / 107 x 122 cm
Courtesy the Helman Collection, New York

35.
Artist's Studio No. 1 (Look Mickey). 1973
Oil, magna and sand on canvas
96 x 128 inches / 244 x 325 cm
Collection Walker Art Center, Minneapolis;
Gift of Judy and Kenneth Dayton and
the T.B. Walker Foundation, 1981

36.
Still Life with Swiss Cheese. 1973
Oil and Magna on canvas
30 x 36 inches / 76 x 91 cm
David Lichtenstein

37.
Stretcher Frame Revealed Beneath
Painting of a Stretcher Frame. 1973
Oil and Magna on canvas
36 x 46 inches / 91 x 117 cm
Private Collection

38.
Entablature. 1974
Magna, aluminum powder, sand
and magna medium on canvas
60 x 100 inches / 152 x 254 cm
Private Collection

39.
Entablature. 1974
Oil and Magna on canvas
60 x 100 inches / 152 x 254 cm
Private Collection

40.
Figures in Landscape. 1977
Oil and Magna on canvas
107 x 166 1/2 inches / 275 x 427 cm
Louisiana Museum of Modern Art

41.
Girl with Tear III. 1977
Oil and Magna on canvas
46 x 40 inches / 117 x 102 cm
Fondation Beyeler, Riehen/Basel

42.
Portrait. 1977
Oil and Magna on canvas
60 x 50 inches / 152 x 127 cm
Private Collection

43.
Cosmology. 1978
Oil and Magna on canvas
107 x 167 1/2 inches / 274 x 429 cm
Private Collection

44.
Self Portrait. 1978
Oil and Magna on canvas
70 x 54 inches / 178 x 137 cm
Private Collection

45.
Flowers. 1982
Magna on canvas
50 x 36 inches / 127 x 91 cm
Private Collection

46.
Painting: Bamboo Frame. 1984
Oil and Magna on canvas
36 x 40 inches / 91 x 102 cm
Private Collection

47.
Painting with Scattered Brushstrokes. 1984
Magna on canvas
50 x 70 inches / 127 x 178 cm
Private Collection

48.
Reflections: Art. 1988
Oil and Magna on canvas
44 1/4 x 76 1/4 inches / 112 x 194 cm
Private Collection

49.
Interior with Exterior (Still Waters). 1991
Oil and Magna on canvas
102 x 173 inches / 259 x 439 cm
Private Collection

50.
Interior with Motel Room Painting. 1992
Oil and Magna on canvas
77 x 96 inches / 196 x 244 cm
Private Collection

51.
Landscape in Fog. 1996
Oil and Magna on canvas
71 x 81 3/4 inches / 180 x 208 cm
Private Collection

52.
Landscape with Boat. 1996
Oil and Magna on canvas
58 3/4 x 96 1/4 inches / 149 x 245 cm
Private Collection

53.
Tall Mountains. 1996
Oil and Magna on canvas
110 x 49 1/4 inches / 279 x 125 cm
Private Collection

54.
Vista with Bridge. 1996
Oil and Magna on canvas
75 x 178 inches / 191 x 452 cm
Private Collection

55.
Interior with Painting of Bather. 1997
Oil and acrylic on canvas
70 x 68 1/2 inches / 178 x 174 cm
The Eli and Edythe L. Broad Collection

DRAWINGS

56.
Bugs Bunny. 1958
India ink on paper
20 x 26 inches / 50.8 x 66 cm
Private Collection

57.
Donald Duck. 1958
India ink on paper
20 1/16 x 26 1/16 inches / 51 x 66.2 cm
Private Collection

58.
Mickey Mouse I. 1958
India ink, pastel and charcoal on paper
19 1/8 x 25 inches / 48.6 x 63.5 cm
Private Collection

59.
Airplane. 1961
Ink on paper
19 3/4 x 21 5/8 inches / 50.2 x 54.9 cm
Sonnabend Collection

60.
Couch. 1961
Ink on paper
19 3/4 x 23 1/4 inches / 50.2 x 59.1 cm
Sonnabend Collection

61.
Girl with Accordion. 1961
Ink on paper
20 1/2 x 18 7/8 inches / 52.1 x 47.9 cm
Sonnabend Collection

62.
Knock Knock. 1961
Ink on paper
20 1/4 x 19 3/4 inches / 51.4 x 50 cm
Sonnabend Collection

63.
Mail Order Foot. 1961
Ink on paper
17 7/8 x 27 1/8 inches / 45.5 x 68.8 cm
Sonnabend Collection

64.
Man with Coat. 1961
Ink on paper
20 1/2 x 19 3/4 inches / 52.1 x 50.2 cm
Sonnabend Collection

65.
Von Karp. 1963
Graphite and coloured pencils on paper
5 3/4 x 5 5/8 inches / 14.6 x 14.3 cm
Private Collection

66.
Drawing for "Girl in Mirror". (1964)
Graphite and coloured pencils on paper
5 3/4 x 5 3/4 inches / 14.6 x 14.6 cm
Private Collection

67.
Drawing for "Nurse". 1964
Graphite and coloured pencils on paper
5 7/8 x 5 15/16 inches / 14.9 x 15.1 cm
Private Collection

68.
Landscape studies. (1964)
Graphite and coloured pencils on paper
4 1/2 x 5 3/4 inches / 11.4 x 14.6 cm
Private Collection

69.
Untitled (Seascape With Clouds). (1964)
Coloured pencils on paper
4 1/4 x 8 inches / 10.8 X 20.3 cm
Private Collection

70.
Brushstroke studies. 1965
India ink and blue marker on paper
26 7/8 x 20 1/8 inches / 68.3 x 51.1 cm
Private Collection

71.
Drawing for "Grrrrrrrrr!". (1965)
Graphite on paper
5 3/4 x 4 1/2 inches / 14.6 x 11.4 cm
Private Collection

72.
Staircase. 1970
Graphite on paper
29 1/4 x 19 3/4 inches / 74.3 x 50.2 cm
Private Collection

73.
Drawing for "Still Life with Mirror". 1972
Graphite and coloured pencils on paper
13 15/16 x 10 15/16 inches / 35.4 x 27.8 cm
Private Collection

74.
Drawing for "Artist's Studio 'Look Mickey'". 1973
Graphite, coloured pencils, paint
and collage on paper
19 1/2 x 24 inches / 49.5 x 61 cm
Roy Lichtenstein Foundation Collection

75.
Drawing for "Fragmented Painting of Lemon
and a Melon on a Table". 1973
Graphite and coloured pencils on paper
10 3/4 x 8 3/8 inches / 27.3 x 21.3 cm
Private Collection

76.
Drawing for "Still Life with Swiss Cheese". 1973
Graphite, coloured pencils and collage on
paper
7 7/8 x 6 15/16 inches / 20 x 17.6 cm
Private Collection

77.
Drawing for "Artist's Studio 'Foot
Medication'". 1974
Graphite, coloured pencils and collage on paper
20 1/8 x 25 inches / 51.1 x 63.5 cm
Private Collection

78.
Drawing for "Figures in Landscape". 1977
Graphite, coloured pencils and
cut-and-pasted paper
12 1/8 x 8 5/8 inches / 30.8 x 21.9 cm
Private Collection

79.
Final drawing for "Figures in Landscape". 1977
Graphite and coloured pencils on paper
13 1/4 x 20 7/8 inches / 33.7 x 53 cm
Whitney Museum of American Art

80.
Drawing for "Portrait". (1977)
Graphite and coloured pencils on paper
5 9/16 x 7 9/16 inches / 14.1 x 19.2 cm
Private Collection

81.
Brushstroke Face. 1987
Graphite, ink and Magna on paper
30 x 20 1/4 inches / 76.2 x 51.4 cm
Private Collection

82.
Drawing for "Nudes in Mirror". 1994
Graphite and coloured pencils on paper
15 x 11 3/8 inches / 38.1 x 28.9 cm
Private Collection

83.
Drawing for "Coup de Chapeau (Self Portrait)".
1995
Graphite and coloured pencils on paper
5 5/8 x 8 1/4 inches / 14.3 x 21 cm
Private Collection

84.
Sketch, Nude on Phone with Bust. 1995
Graphite on paper
9 3/4 x 13 3/8 inches / 24.8 x 34 cm
Private Collection

85.
Study for Chapel of the Eucharist, Padre Pio
Pilgrimage Church. 1997
Graphite and coloured pencils on paper
8 x 8 1/2 inches / 20.3 x 21.6 cm
Private Collection

80.
Drawing for "Portrait". (1977)
Private Collection

79.
Final drawing for
"Figures in Landscape". 1977
Whitney Museum of American Art

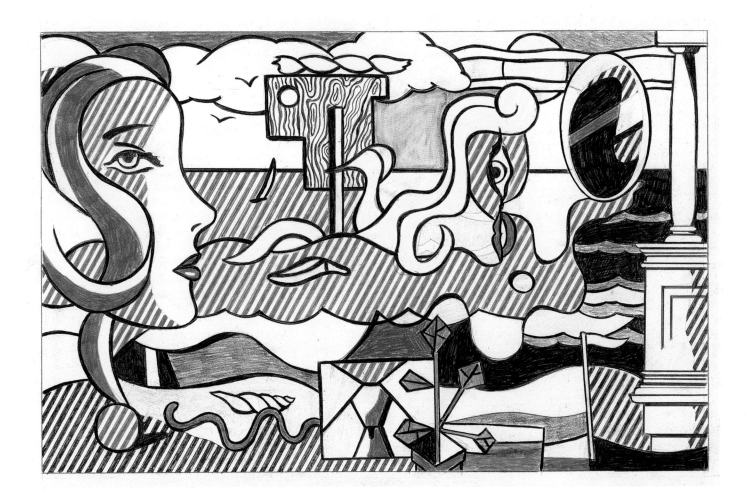

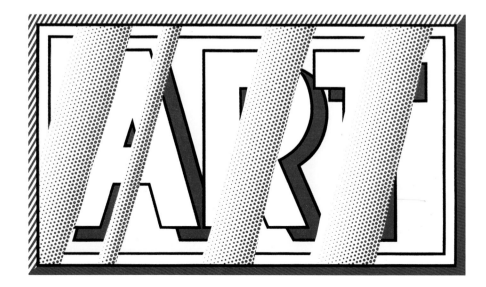